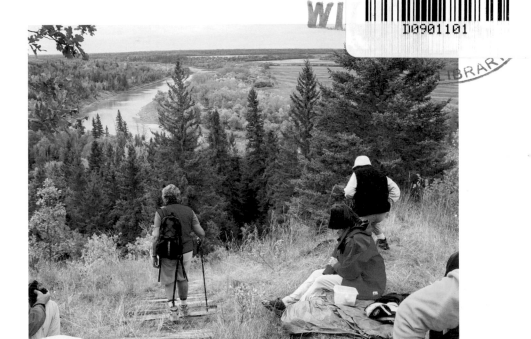

HIKING THE HEARTLAND

Explore Manitoba on foot

by the

Prairie Pathfinders

Hiking the heartland : explore Manitoba on foot
Copyright ©2007 Prairie Pathfinders Inc.

Published by Prairie Pathfinders Inc.
PO Box 68052
RPO Osborne Village
Winnipeg, Manitoba, Canada R3L 2V9

Printed in Canada by City Press
Winnipeg, Manitoba

First Edition
ISBN 978-0-9683976-4-0

Library and Archives Canada Cataloguing in Publication

Hiking the heartland : explore Manitoba on foot / Prairie Pathfinders.
Includes index.
ISBN 0-9683976-4-6
1. Hiking - Manitoba - Guidebooks. 2. Walking - Manitoba - Guidebooks.
3. Trails - Manitoba - Guidebooks. 4. Manitoba - Guidebooks. I. Prairie
Pathfinders (Association)

GV199.44.C32M36 2007   796.51097127
C2007-900523-3

We gratefully acknowledge the financial support provided by the Sustainable Development Innovations Fund, Manitoba Community Services Council, The Burns Family Foundation, Manitoba Heritage Grants Program, Louisiana Pacific Canada Ltd., Rivers West-Red River Corridor Assoc. Ltd., The Frank & Agnes DeFehr Foundation, RBC Foundation, The Wawanesa Mutual Insurance Co. and a grant from the Winnipeg Foundation, a contributor to the quality of life in our community since 1921.

About the authors

For the past decade, Prairie Pathfinders Inc, a non profit group originated by four women (Wendy Wilson, Kathleen Leathers, Sheila Spence & Leone Banks) have devoted their time to the promotion of hiking in Manitoba while showcasing our many beautiful and diverse trails. We take as an article of faith the importance of understanding and caring for nature. But to develop an appreciation of our natural world, we  need to make a real connection. That connection is best made through hiking.

Over the years, we have become determined advocates for hiking in our province. It is now our life's work to share the beauty, the history, and the natural wonders of Manitoba that can best be appreciated on foot. Our dream, which every day is becoming more concrete, is to not only make Manitobans enthusiastic hikers but also to make Manitoba a tourist destination for hiking.

Acknowledgments

During the more than three years that we have worked on this project, we have received help from many people and organizations. We are particularly grateful to the members of the Prairie Pathfinders Walking Club for their encouragement and enthusiastic participation in our outdoor adventures. We would like to single out the following individuals and organizations  for their generous support - George Beaudry, Seta Bernhart, Jim Birnie, Crystal Bishoff, Barry & Lynne Cornish, Jacquie Crone, Gary Dickson, Glenn Fewster, the Fouilard family, Brent Couthro, the Grossart family, Lorna Hendrickson, Heritage Winnipeg, Brian Hunter, Lorne Hyde, Paul Jordan, Sheldon Kowalchuk, Ed Ledohowski, Nicole Legal, Janice Lukes, Manitoba Conservation staff (Ron Bell, Doug Coupland, Rod Noel, Gary Polson, Glen Suggett), Manitoba Historical Society, Ruth Marr, Irma McDougall, Beth McKechnie, Ardythe McMaster, the McPherson family, Dorothy Melikian, Doris Mae Oulton, Millie Reid, Robert Shaw, Marsha Sheppard, Louise Smendziuk, Joan & Frits Stevens, Arda, Douglas & Ella Thomson, Andrew, Sharon & Grace Thomson, Lyn Ward, Harold Westdal, Janet Wilson and Margaret Yorke.

OUT OF THE ORDINARY

Thunder Hill 8
William Lake 10
Hogsback 12
Poole Property 13
Big Rock 14
Top of the World 17
Mars Hills 18
Bellsite... 20
Roseau River 22
St Lupicin / Roseisle....................... 24
Souris Riverbend........................... 26

LEISURELY NATURE HIKES

Hecla Island 28
Pembina Valley............................. 30
Prime Meridian Trail 32
Sandilands 34
Shell River Valley 35
The Beaches 36
Blue Lakes / Shining Stone 38
Clear Lake South 40
Spirit Sands.................................. 42
St Ambrose................................... 44
Pine Point Rapids.......................... 46
Spur Woods.................................. 48
Spruce Grove 49

TERRIFIC TOWN TOURS

Neepawa 50
Flin Flon 52
Carman 54
Pinawa 56
Emerson....................................... 58
Minnedosa.................................... 60
Thompson 62
Morden 64
Portage la Prairie 66
Selkirk 68
Souris 70
Brandon.. 72
Dauphin.. 74
Victoria Beach 76

CHALLENGING DAY HIKES

Centennial Trail 78
Clear Lake North 80
Castle Rock................................... 82
Tinker Creek.................................. 84
South Cypress TCT 85
George Lake 86
Tiger Hills 88
Black Lake..................................... 90
James Lake 92
Grasshopper Valley........................ 94
Elk Island..................................... 96
Gorge Creek.................................. 98
Hunt Lake 100

BACK PACKING

Spruce Woods 102
Kwasitchewan Falls 104
Riding Mountain 106
The Whiteshell 108
Duck Mountains 110

EASY FAMILY WALKS

Baldy Mountain 114
Isputinaw Trail 115
Prairie Shore Nature Trail 116
Karst Springs 117
Boreal Trail 118
Walk On Ancient Mountains 119
Forester's Footsteps 120
Stephenfield 121
Bead Lakes 122
Disappearing Lakes 123
Narcisse Snake Dens 124
Ancient Valley 125
Marshs Lake 126
Wekusko Falls 127
Agassiz Interpretive 128
Spray Lake 129
Clearwater Caves 130
Amisk 131
Fire of 83 132
Copernicus Hill 133

EXPLORING HISTORY HIKES

Silverbend 134
Camp Morton 136
Criddle/Vane Homestead.............. 138
Old Pinawa Dam 141
Asessippi 142
Negrych Homestead 144
Grey Owl's Cabin 146
Old Fort Ellice 148
Bruxelles 150
Stonewall Quarry 152
Hecla Village 153

BACK COUNTRY RAMBLES

Rae Trail 154
Kettle Stones 156
Black Wolf Trail 157
Little Bald Hill 158
Bowsman Overlook 160
National Footpath 162
Roaring River 164
Langford Pasture 166
Brandon Hills 168
Sugarloaf Hills 170
Routledge Sand Hills 172
Lauder Sand Hills 174

HIKING THE HEARTLAND

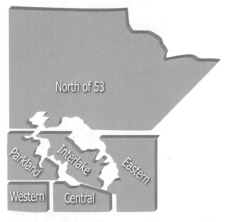

North of 53

Parkland

Interlake

Eastern

Western

Central

EASTERN

Top of the World	17
Mars Hills	18
Spur Woods	48
The Beaches	36
Pine Point Rapids	46
Sandilands	34
Pinawa	56
Victoria Beach	76
Centennial Trail	78
Castle Rock	82
George Lake	86
Black Lake	90
Elk Island	96
Hunt Lake	100
Whiteshell backpacking	108
Walk on Ancient Mountains	119
Forester's Footsteps	120
Amisk Trail	131
Fire of 83	132
Old Pinawa Dam	141

INTERLAKE

Hecla Island	28
Prime Meridian Trail	32
St Ambrose	44
Selkirk	68
Narcisse Snake Dens	124
Camp Morton	136
Stonewall Quarry	152
Hecla Village	153
Black Wolf Trail	157

WESTERN

William Lake	10
Spruce Woods Hogsback	12
Poole Property	13
Souris Riverbend	26
Spirit Sands	42
Neepawa	50
Minnedosa	60
Souris	70
Brandon	72
South Cypress TCT	85
James Lake	92
Spruce Woods backpacking	102
Isputinaw Trail	115
Disappearing Lakes	123
Marshs Lake	126
Silverbend	134
Criddle / Vane Homestead	138
Old Fort Ellice	148
National Footpath	162
Langford Pasture	166
Brandon Hills	168
Routledge Sand Hills	172
Lauder Sand Hills	174

CENTRAL

Roseau River 22
St Lupicin / Roseisle........................ 24
Pembina Valley.............................. 30
Carman 54
Emerson.. 58
Morden 64
Portage la Prairie 66
Tinker Creek.................................... 84
Tiger Hills 88
Prairie Shore Nature Trail 116
Stephenfield 121
Agassiz Interpretive....................... 128
Rae Trail.. 154
Bruxelles 150

PARKLAND

Thunder Hill...................................... 8
Big Rock.. 14
Bellsite.. 20
Shell River Valley 35
Blue Lakes / Shining Stone 38
Clear Lake South 40
Dauphin... 74
Clear Lake North 80
Grasshopper Valley 94
Gorge Creek.................................... 98
Riding Mountain backpacking 106
Duck Mountain backpacking 110
Baldy Mountain 114
Boreal Trail....................................118
Bead Lakes 122
Ancient Valley................................ 125
Spray Lake 129
Copernicus Hill 133
Asessippi....................................... 142
Negrych Homestead 144
Grey Owl's Cabin 146
Kettle Stones................................. 156
Little Bald Hill 158
Bowsman Overlook 160
Roaring River 164
Sugarloaf Hills............................... 170

NORTH OF 53

Flin Flon 52
Thompson 62
Kwasitchewan Falls....................... 104
Karst Springs.................................117
Wekusko Falls............................... 127
Clearwater Caves.......................... 130

distance

4.5 km loop

throughout the west.

Just 100 years ago you would have gazed upon a continuous sea of thick forest stretching off to the horizon instead of the colourful checker board of farmland. Today it is some of the finest agricultural land in the world.

The one constant within the Valley is abundance. In 1898, word of this abundance set off a land rush. The most enterprising souls struggled to stake their homestead claims ahead of the onslaught of settlers that would

some history

Thunder Hill has been a source of wonder and mystery for centuries. Native peoples believed the Great Spirit gave birth to thunder and lightning from its summit. They gave it the name Thunderbird Mountain and were terrified to go near during a storm. Early fur traders shortened the name to Thunder Hill, and as they travelled the Pelly Trail, valued it as an important landmark.

As you stand on top of Thunder Hill looking southeast, you have an important part of our early history within sight. That famous fur trade route, the Pelly Trail, wound through the valley to supply outposts as far afield as Alberta and the U.S. and was a vital passage way for early settlers.

A vivid picture of this area, circa 1800, emerges from the journals of Daniel Harmon. He was a Northwest Company trader stationed near Thunder Hill for years. He writes of ox carts and pack horses, dog sleds and canoes, all hauling abundant riches out of the valley - furs and buffalo robes, timber and pemmican, dried fish and spruce gum. The Native peoples even produced salt and sugar in quantities sufficient to supply forts

Glorious views of the Swan River Valley from the ski lodge and at the so-called 'diamond slide' atop a steep shale embankment where for years, kids have had fun searching for diamond shaped crystals of selenite.

As well, the beautiful bridges and boardwalks that were built over the creeks make this hike memorable.

propositions of about equal appeal. On the advice of his mentor, A J Cotton (whose career we discuss on page 89), he opted for homesteading in the Valley near Thunder Hill. In the end, he made his fortune here, no doubt a greater one than he would have found panning for gold.

come with the railway. One of the first to arrive with his ox and cart, was a young Charlie Banks (grandfather of one of the authors). He had earlier debated heading off for the great Yukon gold rush instead. To him, the lure of gold and the lure of rich farmland were

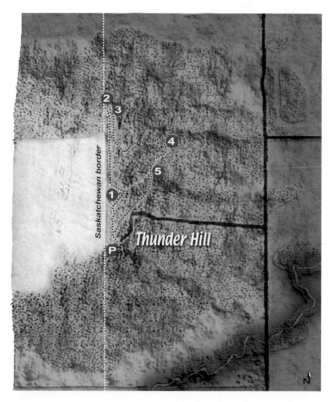

Saskatchewan border

Thunder Hill

WAYPOINTS	
52°1'01.5"N, 101°36'30.7"W	**P** *Park near ski lodge*
52°1'19.6"N, 101°36'25.7"W	**1** *trail intersection*
52°1'47.7"N, 101°36'35.3"W	**2** *overlook / diamond slide*
52°1'45.9"N, 101°36'33.1"W	**3** *trail intersection*
52°1'36.5"N, 101°36'04.8"W	**4** *bridges / boardwalks*
52°1'25.6"N, 101°36'11.6"W	**5** *trail Intersection*

FYI

These trails were developed over the years by a bike club called 'Tread the Thunder'. The club is happy to share with hikers and you'll find signage and a map at the trailhead.

distance

9 km loop

some history

This Turtle Mountain region is the oldest inhabited part of the province. It was the first area to become free of ice cover when glaciers receded 12,000 to 14,000 years ago. Artifacts dating back thousands of years have been found here.

William Lake was named by a party of picnickers who came here in the 1880s. Five men in the group were all named William and so it was decided that this pretty site should share their name.

what's special

One section of this park trail closely follows the shoreline of picturesque William Lake with fine overlooks along the way. Another part climbs the steep Turtle's Back, giving you a panoramic view.

What is most special about this trail, however, is the fact that almost half of it runs through community pasture. Two excellent stair-step stiles take you in and out of this rolling wooded pasture land and offer you a hiking experience that is unique in Manitoba.

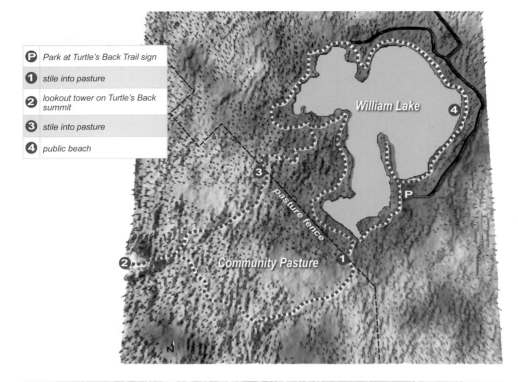

P	*Park at Turtle's Back Trail sign*
1	*stile into pasture*
2	*lookout tower on Turtle's Back summit*
3	*stile into pasture*
4	*public beach*

William Lake

pasture fence

Community Pasture

distance

1.5 km one way /
3 km out & back

how to get there

Take Park Road off Hwy 2 just
east of Cypress River. The road
is fairly good up to the horse
and canoe camping turnoff.
Park and follow the sandy
track east to the Hogsback
overlook.

what you'll find

Expect a panoramic view
of the river valley. Our route
takes you out along the
edge of steep sandy cliffs
and down to the base of
the 'Hogsback' - an unusual
landform created by the
erosion of underground
streams.

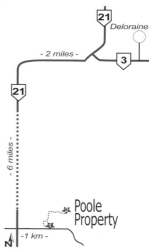

WAYPOINTS	
49°5'17.9"N, 100°32'28.2"W	**P** One mile east of Hwy 21, you'll find a small parking lot beside a cairn
49°5'35.2"N, 100°31'57.1"W	**1** Destination / Overlook

what's special

This short hike gives you some terrific views of the prairie from the western edge of Turtle Mountain. It's a fun place to wander and explore but to help you find your way, the Turtle Mountain Conservation District office has made plans to keep a trail mowed from the cairn to the overlook point.

distance

1.5 km one way / 3 km out & back

some history

This 120 acre parcel of native grassland & hardwood forest was donated to the Turtle Mountain Conservation District by the late William R Poole. It was his dying wish that the natural characteristics of the land be preserved and that hikers be encouraged to enjoy this beautiful property.

what's special

These are the highest (65 feet), most dramatic and most beautiful cliffs that you can hike to in Manitoba. They make the more famous and much photographed Steep Rock cliffs look puny by comparison.

You have two spectacular views - one overlooking Dawson Bay from the top of the cliffs and another from the shoreline looking up at our own 'Mount Rushmore'.

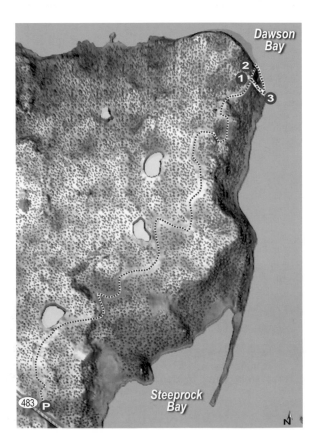

some history

These cliffs were created from shells deposited in layers 300 million years ago when this area was covered by a shallow sea. The yellow & white Devonian limestone and dolomite are beautifully stratified and some bands contain a large number of fossils. Ripple marks near the top give evidence of waves acting on an ancient sea shore.

WAYPOINTS		
52°47'51.2"N, 100°59'05.7"W	**P**	*Park off the road*
52°50'56.8"N, 100°55'49.5"W	**1**	*turn-off to cliff trail*
52°51'04.7"N, 100°55'42.7"W	**2**	*cliff overlook*
52°50'51.6"N, 100°55'37.7"W	**3**	*path down to water*

FYI

As Hwy 483 is a busy road, it's best to park well off to the side. The trail is on a well-defined ATV track. Expect easy hiking except for the mud holes.

This land is owned by Sapotaweyak Cree Nation. Before starting your hike you'll need to ask permission from Councillor Nelson Genaille 204.734-8584.

distance

10 km one way / 20 km out & back

(This is the distance to the overlook. Add approx 3 km to climb down the cliffs & hike along the shore & return)

distance

2 km one way /
4 km out & back

how to get there

From the parking lot of the Falcon Trails Resort, follow signage to the trail system. The first part of the route goes south on a service road. Signage will direct you to the 'Top of the World' overlook. It used to be known as 'The Cliff'.

what's special

The overlook is the highest elevation in the area with a lovely view of Falcon Lake

Falcon Lake

Falcon Trails Resort

Falcon Lake

Southshore Rd

what's special

Wild flowers grow in abundance, and a trembling aspen and jack pine forest provide shade and shelter for the maze of sandy trails.

distance

10 km loop

59 | Libau | 317 | Mars Sand Hills | 12 | N

some history

The Mars Hills Wildlife Management Area is a tangle of sandy trails and cart tracks winding for miles through a mix of woodland and open meadow. This is a popular area. You can come across people picking berries or mushrooms or digging for seneca root. Orienteering, horseback riding, bird watching, cross country skiing - these all coexist quite nicely with the odd ATV or dirt bike. This is a freewheeling place.

The scars from old 'quarried out' gravel pits are a fact of life here. You'll encounter several on the trail. It is heartening, however, when nature and/or man works at restoring life to these 'decommissioned' pits.

The Mars Hills are part of a complex

FYI

Park off the road near the golf course sign. We've put up some Prairie Pathfinder markers on the trail but we have no trailhead sign. You may see a 'Trans Canada Trail' sign nearby, but it has nothing to do with our route.

It's easy to become disoriented in here and you'd be well advised to carry a GPS or at least a compass.

series of sandy end-moraine ridges which stretch all the way from Victoria Beach south through the Sandilands Provincial Forest. An end-moraine is the deposit left by a glacier that stood in one place for many years. Unlike most moraines, however, the Mars Hills are made up largely of clean sand and gravel and have very little clay or silt. This is because the glacial deposits were washed clean by melt water flowing deposition. In this way the lighter weight silts and clays typically found in end moraines were carried away. For this reason, the Mars Hills are an exceptional source of premium sand and gravel.

WAYPOINTS

50°15'54.0"N, 96°35'03.4"W	**P** Park off the road
50°15'14.1"N, 96°35'52.9"W	**1** trail intersection
50°15'07.8"N, 96°36'11.0"W	**2** decommissioned gravel pit
50°14'30.2"N, 96°36'42.6"W	**3** trail intersection
50°14'37.1"N, 96°35'36.0"W	**4** trail intersection
50°14'37.6"N, 96°35'09.2"W	**5** trail intersection

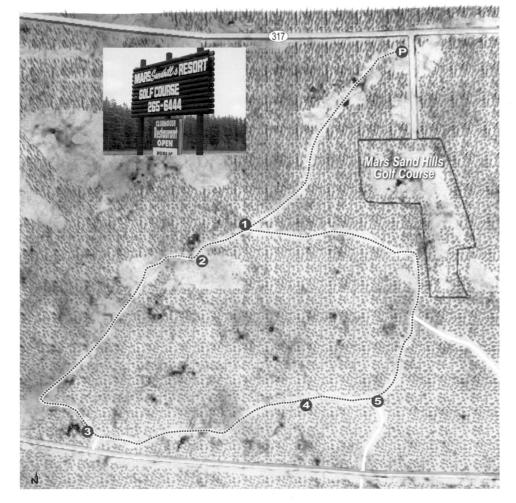

to Mafeking

10

Bellsite
Trail

- 1.5 km -

Bell River

Turn-off
to
Bellsite

to
Birch River

N

distance

7 km one way /
14 km out & back

how to get there

Find a side road running east into the Porcupine Prov Forest, 1.5 km north of the Bellsite turn-off. The condition of this road will depend on the amount of logging being done in this area. Drive in as far as is practical and park well off the side of the road.

what's special

You are ascending the northern end of the Manitoba Escarpment through dense mixed forest. Whatever effort is required to trudge up these steep slopes is amply rewarded with glorious views from the top. Our destination is a narrow foot path (along a Hogsback land form) out to a Bell River Canyon overlook.

some history

The trail is an old logging road that was probably cut around 1900. Back then, logging was an important part of the lives of everyone in the area. At its peak, thousands of men found employment in the Porcupine logging camps and saw mills.

The largest lumber enterprise in the Valley was the Burrows Lumber Company. At one time, T.A. Burrows held under license practically all spruce timber in the Porcupine

and Duck Mountains.

These logging roads could be especially treacherous in winter. Teams of horses hauled huge water tanks up and down, icing the roads into sleigh runs. One winter day in the 1920s, so the story goes, Mr. Burrows had the fright of his life. He was being driven up to a camp in a new Model T. Ford when a massive wagon load of logs came thundering down the slopes toward them. The noise of the car motor prevented their hearing its approach until the very last second. It was only with quick manoeuvring and the greatest luck, that disaster was narrowly averted, but Burrows was never the same and his faith in modern technology was badly shaken.

FYI

Much of this trail is on a logging road that may still be in use and its condition fluctuates depending on the amount of logging activity - especially over the first few miles. As of 2006, it has mainly fallen into disrepair.

Beaver pond

Bellsite Trail Hogsback overlook

WAYPOINTS

52°36'09.4"N, 101°5'54.2"W	**P**	*Park to the side of the road*
52°35'26.0"N, 101°7'00.9"W	**1**	*turn-off*
52°35'42.2"N, 101°8'04.6"W	**2**	*bridge*
52°35'59.5"N, 101°8'44.1"W	**3**	*beaver pond*
52°35'51.5"N, 101°9'04.4"W	**4**	*turn-off to hogsback trail*
52°35'36.9"N, 101°8'57.5"W	**5**	*Hogsback overlook / destination*

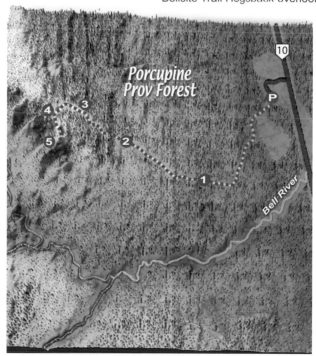

Porcupine
Prov Forest

Bell River

what's special

The suspension bridge is a delight and the dramatic sandy cliffs that the Roseau River has carved out over the centuries are quite a surprise.

some history

This trail is an old school path that leads down to the river from the now deserted hamlet of Senkiw. In years gone by children who lived on the south side, crossed the river in a cable basket that they pulled by hand from one side to the other. In 1946, farm families got together and built this wonderful foot bridge. It was a unique design and made heavy use of discarded farm machinery in its construction.

The bridge fell into disuse when the school closed in the 60s but in the last few years, the community has once again come together to restore the bridge to its former glory. This site has now become something of a tourist destination. On a summer weekend you'll find people fishing, having picnics and just enjoying the great fun of scooting across the swinging bridge.

distance

5 km one way /
10 km out & back

Rosa

Senkiw

59

Senkiw
Foot
Bridge

- 1 mi -

- 2 mi -

Roseau River

Roseau
River

N

how to get there

You can reach this trailhead from different directions but the map above shows the most straight forward route. Find the road running west (about .75 km north of Roseau River.) Follow it for 2 miles, then turn north for 1 mile, then west again. All that remains of the town of Senkiw are a few old buildings that are mainly abandoned. Park to the side of the road and look for TCT direction signs - this trail is part of the Trans Canada Trail.

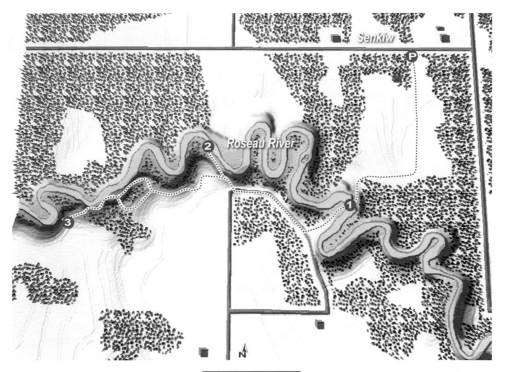

WAYPOINTS

49°12'26.8"N, 96°52'37.0"W	**P**	Senkiw townsite / Park to the side of the road
49°11'53.9"N, 96°52'59.2"W	**1**	suspension bridge
49°12'07.2"N, 96°53'47.0"W	**2**	Roseau River ford site
49°11'50.5"N, 96°54'33.3"W	**3**	overlook & turn-around point

distance

12.5 km loop

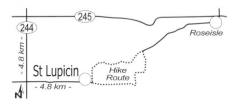

some history

St Lupicin was a sizable French speaking parish town in the early 1900s. Now most of the buildings are gone. The spire of the Roman Catholic church that peeks over the treetops is now a private residence. The desertion of the town populace was almost complete in the early 1970s when the valley was 're-discovered'. An eclectic group of individuals that the locals considered 'hippies' or 'flower children' decided to make this rugged and beautiful area their home. Whatever their label, these new settlers put

what you'll find

Our route takes twisting dirt and gravel roads up and down the steep valley walls of Snow Valley, offering up great views of the escarpment along the way.

down roots in the valley and brought with them many artistic talents along with their counter-culture views. Today the area is famous for this group of artisans settled in these hills.

This tight-knit enclave of new residents is a very private group. As you walk along you wouldn't guess how many homes are tucked up in the hills. The only evidence of their presence is the profusion of 'no trespassing' posters. Given their undisputed anti-establishment history, there is some irony in the wealth

that the route is entirely on public property.

One historically interesting site that is in full view along our route, is the remains of the ❶ Leary Brick Factory. It was one of dozens of brick factories operated in Manitoba, many dating back to the 1890s and nearly all in the south central region where clay deposits are common. After the first world war, a downturn in the economy and the availability of less expensive brick from outside the province spelled the end of these enterprises. Learys is the only factory site

with buildings still standing to this day. Interestingly, Leary descendants now live in the brick house adjacent to the old factory site.

of 'private property' signs plastered along the roadside. Take comfort from the fact

what's special

Standing on the grassy edge of a height of land, one looks far down to where a gleaming ribbon of water turns abruptly northward and weaves its way through the dramatic Souris River Valley.

This valley is a legacy of a channel that thousands of years ago linked the Souris and Pembina valleys. Souris River Bend is a compelling landscape of deep ravines, gullies and lush benchlands. The habitat is diverse. Maple and elm forests shade the riverbanks; mixed-grass prairie of spear grass and bluestem grasses blanket the terraces; aspen and bur oak cluster along the ravines.

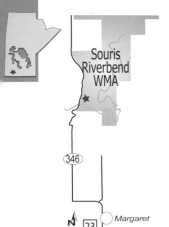

distance

11 km loop

some history

One of the trails we find in this Wildlife Management Area, is the Lang Trail, which is part of the historic Mandan Trail. Ancient cart tracks lead down to Lang's Crossing on the Souris River. We read of this ford as early as 1806 when Alexander Henry trekked through this part of the country. This was long before James Lang took up his homestead here in 1880. Lang became an important person to the settlers travelling along the trail because he always stocked extra supplies for their needs. For this reason, the ford and the valley bear his name.

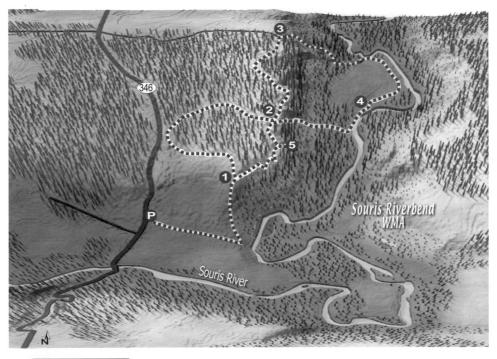

Frits Stevens

Frits Stevens

WAYPOINTS

49°28'02.8"N, 99°52'10.4"W	**P**	*Park to the side of the road*
49°28'18.3"N, 99°51'43.5"W	**1**	*trail intersection*
49°28'37.9"N, 99°51'29.0"W	**2**	*trail intersection*
49°29'15.0"N, 99°51'26.9"W	**3**	*trail intersects with road*
49°28'47.4"N, 99°50'49.2"W	**4**	*riverside overlook / campsite*
49°20'22.5"N, 99°51'32.1"W	**5**	*valley overlook*

how to get there

Our starting point is about 9 km north of the town of Margaret on Hwy 346. Turn east off the road onto a cart track that you'll find approx. 0.75 km north of the river.

FYI

Within the WMA, 40 km of equestrian trails have been surveyed and marked by the Distance Riders of Manitoba. You'll find a large billboard map of these trails on your route. Hikers are welcome on this system of trails.

distance

9 km loop

what's special

Our route loops the north shoreline of historic Hecla Island serving up picture postcard views of towering limestone cliffs and white sand beaches. This island seems oddly out of place on the Prairies, more at home on the Atlantic coast with its quaint lighthouses, bobbing fishing boats and pelicans wheeling overhead. Our route showcases the many attractions of this popular tourist destination. Beginning at the marina we hike past swimming beaches, campgrounds, and picnic sites, later trailing past a world-class golf course and the landscaped gardens of the newly refurbished Hecla Oasis Resort. Another highlight follows a narrow penisula out to the beautiful Lighthouse Trail.

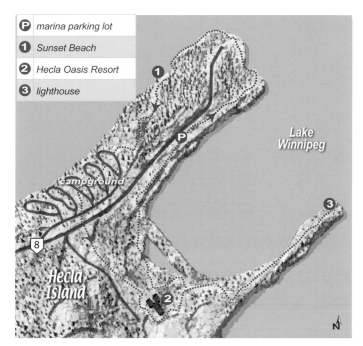

P marina parking lot
1 Sunset Beach
2 Hecla Oasis Resort
3 lighthouse

Lake Winnipeg

campground

8

Hecla Island

N

Christel Bischoff

what's special

This is our only park in the Pembina Hills and its creation in 2001 helped Manitoba expand its network of protected areas. Although relatively small in size, Pembina Valley Park is still very important in that it links the Pembina Valley WMAs and the Pembina Valley Camp. These three parcels of land combine to form one large habitat area for the wildlife and plants that live there. Because farmland and towns cover much of southern Manitoba, the value of these natural lands holds even greater significance.

The hiking trails are exceptionally fine. Serving up panoramic valley views along the way, they cross boulder-filled creeks and wind up and down steep valleys walls through dense aspen and oak forest and out onto the broad expanse of Deer Meadow.

some history

As you look out over this wide valley, you may be struck by an apparent discrepancy. How was this massive valley formed by such a narrow trickle of water? The answer goes back thousands of years to when the earth began to warm after the last Ice Age and melting glaciers produced enormous torrents of raging water. An ancient river that was miles wide cut out the valley walls you see before you.

Special credit for his critical role in the establishment of this park must go to one individual. Henry Martens bought up this land with the aim of sharing his beautiful Pembina Valley with the rest of the world. For years, Martens had a vision of creating the 'Eureka Valley Interpretive Centre' and using his own equipment, he cut a network of trails.

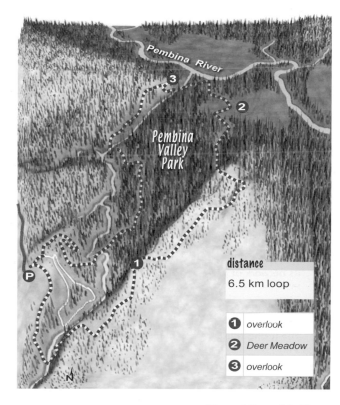

Pembina River

Pembina Valley Park

3 overlook

2 Deer Meadow

1 overlook

distance

6.5 km loop

N

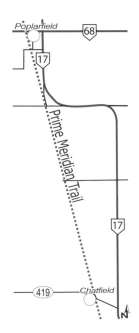

distance

12 km one way / 24 km out & back
We recommend hiking one way by taking two vehicles and leaving one at either trailhead.

some history

The Interlake is a land of limestone. It underlies the entire region, frustrating land drainage. In many areas it breaks through the blanket of glacial till that itself is mainly composed of limestone minerals. The thin stoney soil throughout this region holds only the bleakest prospects for grain production.

Between 1906 and 1912, a flood of immigrants from the western Ukraine took up farming here. They were Galician peasants for the most part, and in their native land, had been subject to the oppressions of autocratic regimes for generations. Land of their own, no matter what the quality, was a gift from heaven. This attitude would serve them well because their only bumper crop would be rocks. Not easily deterred, they struggled to clear the bush for garden and pasture but after a generation or two of bravely challenging this land, most gave up the losing battle and moved on.

This trail is named for and runs near the Principal Meridian, which is an important line of reference as the starting point of the entire land survey of western Canada. From Poplarfield to Chatfield you'll pass through countryside that is primarily wilderness with areas of open meadow and mixed forest. Deep Lake (a marsh with a one mile long stretch of open water) is about midpoint on the trail and makes a strategic location for a rest stop.

Poplarfield has two historic churches worth checking out. One is the St Nicholas Ukrainian Catholic Church built in 1913. Tiny Chatfield is a delightful stroll down memory lane. Be sure to stop for a tour of the old pool hall / barber shop with its gold mine of vintage memorabilia from the community's past.

distance

6.5 km loop

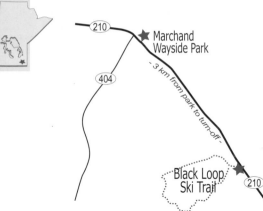

some history

The Sandilands Provincial Forest is a vast tract of land reserved to grow trees for our forest industry. It is an added benefit that we can hike, ski, cycle and snowmobile here in this beautiful pine forest.

Economically speaking, Sandilands is one of the most valuable forest reserves in Manitoba due to its location near markets in Winnipeg and pulp and paper mills at Pine Falls. Extensive logging has gone on here since the 1890s and the forest has been entirely disturbed by either fires or timber harvesting. There are few stands of natural mature trees.

One reason for the early, intensive logging was the railway line that was built into Marchand in 1898, making logging and transporting timber very economical. The 'Muskeg Special', as it was nicknamed, was built by railway entrepreneurs MacKenzie & Mann, and no sooner had they pulled into the station than their cars were filled with cord wood. It was a profitable venture for all concerned. Eventually, the rail line was pushed through to Port Arthur, opening up even more lucrative markets.

Over the years, Sandilands became badly overharvested and needed to be saved. In 1912, the first forest ranger in western Canada was assigned here, and in 1923, the Sandilands became a forest reserve. Today, forest management is government controlled and foresters are expected to not only grow trees but nurture the entire forest ecosystem. The practice of cultivating a forest is termed 'silviculture'. A forester is to silviculture what a farmer is to agriculture.

If you're not bothered by the fact that this is not a pristine wilderness, you'll find this a great place to hike all year round. The trails are popular with snowmobilers who don't mind sharing with hikers. The snowmobile traffic packs down the snow making it a great winter walk.

distance

4.5 km loop

what you'll find

This park trail leads hikers through forest covering, a meadow, past the Shell River and through a calcium bog. A fairly steep climb to a viewpoint will reward hikers with a spectacular view of the Shell River valley.

During the day you may see elk beds in the meadow.

Ancient Beach Trail

Grand Beach Prov Park

Lake Winnipeg

★ Ancient Beach Trail

Grand Beach Prov Park

East Park Gate

59

12

N

some history

Grand Beach is one of the finest beaches in the entire world. With its miles of powdery white sand, it's no surprise that thousands of sun worshippers gather here every summer. This is our most popular summer destination and has been a mecca for young people for almost a hundred years. Back in the 1920s, they came up from Winnipeg by train. In those days this was a full-fledged resort town with a real carnival atmosphere. There were two key places to see and be seen. One was the boardwalk that extended from the train station to the east lagoon, and then there was the famous dance pavilion. It attracted a great swarm of young people every night of the week all summer long. The CN ran a 'midnight special' out from the city every evening. After a night of dancing, the party crowd would return home

distance

6 km loop

by moonlight. Today, the dance hall is gone and the boardwalk diminished, but this is still the capital of summertime fun for many thousands of Manitobans.

Leave the raucous fun-seekers behind and head into the quiet trails of the Ancient Beach Ridge trail system. These sandy slopes scattered with granite boulders are part of the Belair moraine, a hill-like landform deposited here by glacial activity more than 14,000 years ago. You'll reach a height of land that offers a glorious view of Lake Winnipeg, and as you climb through aspen, birch and jack pine, you'll cross three distinct shorelines of long-gone Lake Agassiz.

The trail leading down to the north takes you to Lester Beach. You'll reach a vehicle barricade and follow the main road a short distance until you reach a creek. Here you'll follow a pathway to the left or west, down to the public beach. Lester Beach presents a more peaceful atmosphere than its raucous neighbour to the south. The serene beauty of its rocky cliffs make this one of Lake Winnipeg's most majestic stretches of shoreline.

what's special

From the bustle and exuberance of glorious Grand Beach - our most famous strip of sand, you'll walk up to the quiet stillness of an ancient beach ridge and then down to sedate Lester Beach with its beautiful cliffs towering overhead. This hike is a study in contrasts.

how to get there

Find the trailhead for the Ancient Beach Trail at the west end of the park.

P	Ancient Beach Trail
1	overlook
2	ski shelter

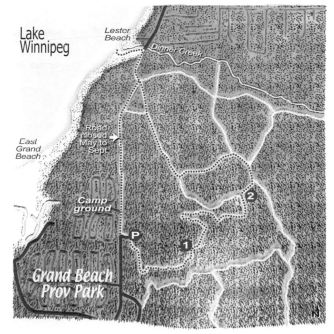

some history

These trails are situated on a peninsula formed thousands of years ago, a remnant of the last great Ice Age. This protruding peninsula consists of a thick layer of glacial debris (boulders, gravel, clay) over a finger-shaped bedrock ridge. At 30 metres higher than West Blue Lake, the crest of the peninsula offers an excellent view.

The clear waters of West Blue Lake reach a depth of up to 37 metres. The lake has no permanent inlets or outlets and is fed by freshwater springs on the lake bottom. Vegetation on the lakeshore reduces bank erosion, thus less soil enters the water. A combination of freshwater springs and reduced bank erosion helps maintain the lake's cold, clear water. Creatures like the lake trout depend on clarity and cool temperatures to survive.

At the southern end of the loop, you'll see a path out to a bench overlooking tiny Lake Shilliday. Named for Sergeant Robert Shilliday who died at age 19 when his plane was shot down over Germany in World War II, this peaceful spot has a very special meaning for his family. In 1988, the ashes of Shilliday's mother were scattered on this lake so that she might 'spend eternity' with this lasting symbol of her beloved son.

distance

Blue Lakes 5.5km loop / Shining Stone 1.1km loop

what's special

These 2 trails are well designed to take advantage of rocky terrain, majestic forest and an almost continuous view of sparkling blue water.

some history

Easily our most beautifully designed townsite, Wasagaming in Riding Mountain National Park is picture-perfect and a world-class tourist destination. Walks, boulevards, and stone-and-log buildings harmonize with the natural beauty of the surroundings. On the lake shore, a large park area has been set out with walkways, pergolas and colourful beds of flowers.

The resort was developed in the 1930s during the Great Depression. Work crews hired through a federal relief program included hundreds of unemployed men from the Scandinavian communities south of the park. These immigrant craftsmen masterfully constructed a number of log buildings, expressive of their home country architecture. Several of these log structures remain and give the town a distinctive rustic flavour.

distance

7.5 km one way / 15 km out & back

what you'll find

For the most part, this path runs very close to the water's edge and offers dazzling views of the lake. Expect some steep descents, sand bars and bridges.

Taking the park visitor centre as your starting point, head west along a beach trail past the tennis courts, then past the mobile home park to the boat launch. The trail from here is marked for hiking. You'll cross a sandy ridge separating Clear Lake from South Lake - a former bay of Clear Lake. This stretch is full of bird life in summer, but high water can present problems.

The trail continues to skirt the shoreline through birch and aspen forest, past a number of church camps and a public swimming area known as the Frith Beach. As you head north along the west side of the lake you'll cross a marsh area on a wooden bridge and come out at the Camp Wannakumbac Conference Center. This is your destination and turn-around point.

P	*Wasagaming Visitor Centre*
1	*boat launch*
2	*Frith Beach*
3	*Camp Wannacumbac*

Spruce Woods
Prov Park

5 Assiniboine River

Spirit Sands
Trail

N

Frits Stevens

what's special

This is a hike through spectacular moving sand dunes, the park's most fascinating and fragile feature. There are a few places in Canada and nowhere else in Manitoba with such large stretches of open sand. Trail signs along the way describe the land, the life that it supports, and the cultural history of Spirit Sands.

some history

To understand the origins of the Spruce Woods landscape, you need to go back 20,000 years when all of Manitoba was

best time to go

Avoid hot weather. This trail can be a 'scorcher'. Spring and fall are great times to be here. On hot summer days, try for an early morning or late evening hike.

covered by a blanket of glacial ice more than 2 km thick. As the huge sheets of ice gradually thawed, a wide melt stream flowed into the ancient Lake Agassiz, dropping silt, sand and gravel along a pathway centred roughly on what is now the Assiniboine River. As you look out over the enormous river valley today, you can imagine the mighty river it once was.

Sand deposits were up to 200 feet deep and covered 6500 square km in a fan-shaped area stretching as far east as Portage la Prairie. Exposure to strong winds heaped the sand into active dunes - a barren sea of shifting sand. Gradually, sufficient moisture encouraged the growth of plant life, disguising the wind-shaped dunes with an overlay of rich vegetation.

In 1806 the fur trader Alexander Henry wrote about those dunes calling them Devil's Mountain. "Many extraordinary stories are related of this mountain, both by Indians and Canadians, of the strange noises heard in its bowels, and the nightly apparitions seen at one particular place ... In crossing those hills our horses sank up to their knees in many places."

The Aboriginal people who came this way believed the dunes were created by Kiche Manitou (the Great Spirit) and so treated the area as sacred, performing rituals when they approached. The name "Spirit Sands" recognizes the dunes' religious significance to early inhabitants.

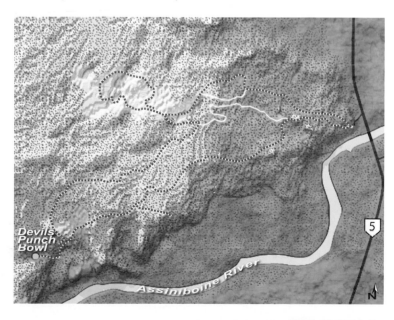

distance

10 km loop

bombardier across the lake to set their nets to catch pickerel and whitefish.

Sixty years ago the Delta Marsh was home to lavish shooting lodges where celebrities and movie stars like Clark Gable and Roy Rogers would come to hunt waterfowl. It was here that various Metis clans developed an international reputation as outfitters and hunting guides. A Metis guide was a major status symbol!

some history

Lake Manitoba is one of the world's largest and shallowest lakes but the waters of this south basin are becoming deeper over time. The last ice age which saw this area buried under glaciers up to four km in depth, depressed the land as much as 1000 metres. With the retreat of these ice sheets 10,000 years ago, the land surface has been rebounding as much as half a metre over 100 years. Since the glacier was thickest in the north, more rebound occurs at the northern end of the lake. Lake Manitoba is much like a bathtub being tipped up with the water slowly deepening at its south end.

St. Ambroise, like St. Laurent and other tiny communities alongside the Delta marsh, was settled by clans of Metis buffalo hunters. Today many residents are commercial fishermen and in winter, they travel by

distance

3.5 km one way / 7 km out & back

what's special

This is Manitoba beachcombing at its best and a birder's paradise. The beautiful sandy shore goes on for miles and the vast adjacent marshland is one of the world's most significant breeding and staging areas for water birds such as grebes, geese, and ducks. As well, some 25 species of warblers migrate here in spectacular flocks, attracted to the wooded beach ridge. The area is also frequented by the piping plover, an extremely rare species of bird that nests in the sand. Parts of the beach may have restricted access from May to July to reduce disturbance to piping plover nests.

Lake
Manitoba

★

*St Ambrose
Prov Park*

430

26

430

Portage la
Prairie

1

N

Lake
Manitoba

Sioux
Pass
Marsh

1 P

2

N

🅿 Park in the picnic area at the
west end of the park

❶ St Ambrose beach

❷ Clandeboye Channel

what's special

Pine Point is a very popular trail through a lush forest of tall spruce and jackpine. A fairly short hike of 3.6 km takes you out to a spectacular rapids where you can picnic beside the rushing water.

distance

8.2 km loop

Whiteshell Prov Park

307
Pine Point Rapids Trail
309
44
44
1
N

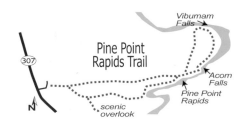

Viburnam Falls

Pine Point Rapids Trail

307

Acorn Falls

Pine Point Rapids

N

scenic overlook

what you'll find

The Whiteshell River gushes over a bed of granite in a series of rapids before subsiding in a quiet pool. The view is breathtaking and the 'young at heart' love sliding in the rushing water.

Pine Point Rapids is an 8.2 km. trail that passes between two sharply different communities typical to the Whiteshell: a mixed-wood forest and a rock outcrop. You will see jack pine, blueberries, sumac, lichens, bur oak, dogwood and cranberry among many others. White-tailed deer, waterfowl and turtles are some of the wildlife you may sight. This is a great trail to take your

hot dogs and marshmallows, as fire pits are provided.

some history

The Spur Woods Wildlife Management Area was established primarily to protect stands of old growth red pine and white cedar. Much credit is owed to the local townspeople of Piney who lobbied long and hard to make this a forest preserve. The Spur Woods Forest attracts hunters and berry-pickers from across the province and the northern United States.

distance

7.5 km loop

what you'll find

Our route follows a sandy track down to an abandoned rail line trail. The sandy upland areas are covered with red and jack pine, white spruce, balsam fir and poplar, with jack pine being the dominant tree. The openness under the canopy provides a great view of these magnificent trees.

The low marshy cedar bog which extends southward from the ridge to the Minnesota border, has many of Manitoba's finest specimens of white cedar; some are 200 years old and more than 200 cm in circumference. Beneath the towering trees grow huge ostrich ferns, wild columbine and the highly prized lady slipper. In spring low lying wet areas produce marsh marigolds in abundance.

WAYPOINTS

49°5'22.1"N, 96°6'48.4"W	**P** park / begin hike
49°4'53.9"N, 96°6'18.2"W	**1** trail intersection
49°4'44.0"N, 96°6'13.3"W	**2** trail intersects w abandoned rail line
49°4'35.2"N, 96°4'48.5"W	**3** trail intersection / turn north

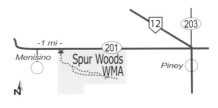

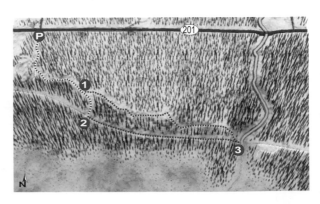

what you'll find

This self-guided trail loops through a stand of black spruce where dense upper branches block sunlight from reaching the forest floor. Points of interest along this trail include a limestone ridge, orchids, "ant city" and a willow grove. The picnic grounds, a log cabin shelter and observation tower with viewing platform round out the Interlake Forest Centre that was developed to promote forestry education and conservation.

The exotic showy lady slipper and calypso orchid thrive in the slightly acid soil of this damp and shady forest. Hunt for them in early June but remember they shouldn't be picked.

distance

1.2 km loop

what's special

The Spruce Grove Nature Trail winds down a ridge into a shady black spruce forest where banks of brilliant green moss and exotic calypso orchids may startle your senses.

Hodgson

17

- 9 km -

233

Fisher
Branch

N

Margaret Laurence House

distance

9 km loop

Stone Angel in Riverside Cemetery

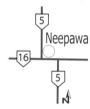

some history

Neepawa proclaims itself 'Manitoba's Most Beautiful Town' and it may well be. But what attracts visitors from as far away as Japan and India isn't its canopy of elm trees and colourful flower beds. It is instead the town's most famous native - world renowned author, Margaret Laurence. Laurence spent the first 18 years of her life in this prairie town and stored up enough memories and impressions to recreate Neepawa as the fictional town of Manawaka in five classic works of Canadian literature. In 1964, Laurence published 'The Stone Angel', followed two years later by 'A Jest of God'. These were the first in a series of powerful and acclaimed novels set in fictional Manawaka, Manitoba. Manawaka was clearly Neepawa - a realization disconcerting to some of its residents, given Laurence's candour and lack of sentimentality about small town life. Yet Neepawa was where Margaret Laurence had grown up and through her it acquired literary immortality. Fans who come to seek out the landmarks and ghosts that inhabit the Laurence landscape will not be disappointed.

The town is nicely situated on a high plateau overlooking a pretty valley where Stoney and Boggy creeks unite to form the Whitemud River. Its old brick buildings on quiet tree-lined streets, exude a sense of pride, prosperity and permanence - a carrying-on of the values of the town's Scots and Presbyterian settlers.

Riverside Cemetery is one of the best known cemeteries in Canada as it is the location of the famous Stone Angel Memorial. This beautifully carved figure, leaning on a cross and holding a wreath, served as inspiration for Laurence's book of the same name and is one of the town's most recognizable symbols. Margaret Laurence's modest gravestone stands nearby on a peaceful hill overlooking the Whitemud River.

Another very powerful symbol here is the lily. If you do this walk in July or August, you'll be astounded by the

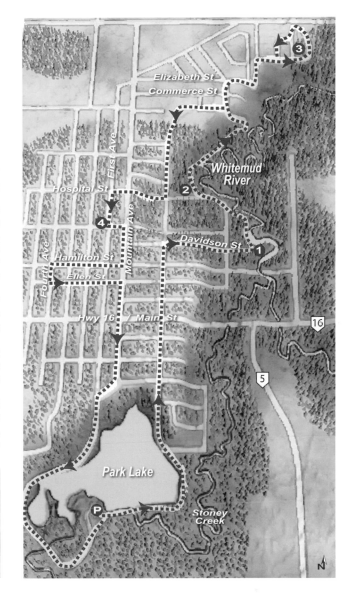

P	*Park Lake parking lot*
1	*Riverbend Park*
2	*community pathway*
3	*Riverside Cemetery*
4	*Margaret Laurence House*

explosion of beautiful blooms in gardens all along the route. The Lily Nook located a couple of miles south of town is a successful commercial venture, growing more than 2000 varieties of bulbs and shipping them all over the world. Visitors are welcome.

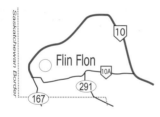

Flin Flon

Saskatchewan Border

10

10A

291

167

what's special

This recently constructed community pathway has to take the prize as the most beautifully designed town trail in the province. It's certainly a boon to Flin Flon residents who were out in force on the day we were there.

Aside from the scenic beauty, you have historic attractions along the way including the natural beauty of rock formations that were formed almost two billon years ago by underwater volcanoes.

some history

Not many years ago, this pretty town perched on a roller coaster of rock was a blighted landscape. As the massive smokestack dominating the skyline suggests, mining is king in Flin Flon. The town was established to service the Hudson Bay Mining and Smelting Company in the 1930s. Years of sulphur dioxide emissions from the smelting complex battered the landscape and it didn't help that early residents cut down most of the trees for firewood and lumber.

The Flin Flon of today is going through an extraordinary rebirth. In 2000, local activists looked at all the bare rock and saw a way to turn things around. They started what they call The Green Project. School children and all interested residents began spreading limestone on small parcels of the barren sites around the town. When crushed and applied to soil acidified by sulphur dioxide emissions, limestone neutralizes the acidity, The soil can then start supporting natural

ground cover. Today birches, willows, poplars and tiny spruce and pine seedlings are now growing on terrain that's been barrren for decades.

distance

4.4 km return

1 *Flinty's Boardwalk*

2 *Ross Lake Trail stairs*

3 *scenic overlook*

how to get there

Find & park beside the 'Flinty's Boardwalk' sign in the middle of town off Hwy 10A.

some history

Carman was one of the first areas settled in southern Manitoba. The Metis established a settlement east of town where the Missouri Trail, a famous early settlement route, forded the Boyne River. These first settlers named the river "La Riviere Isle du Bois" for the bluffs of Manitoba maples that supplied them with sugar and maple syrup each spring. When Ontario settlers moved here in the early 1880s, they renamed the river Boyne and the settlement became 'Carman' as a tribute to an Episcopalian bishop who had honoured the pioneer community with a visit.

Carman can claim distinction for its rich farmland and conservative politics. Included in its list of famous citizens are the 'capital C' conservative Roblin family. Patriarch Sir Rodmond Roblin, one of our province's most colourful politicians, served as premier of Manitoba from 1900 to 1915 and grandson Duff held that title from 1958 to 1967. Rodmond's career was hit by financial scandal over the construction of the Legislative Building, and he was forced to resign. He also had the dubious distinction of being the target of Nellie McClung's sharp satire for

what's special

Carman may be the most nicely treed townsite in Manitoba and its community pathway is a vital pedestrian link between residential areas and the central shopping district and Carman's famous golf course and park.

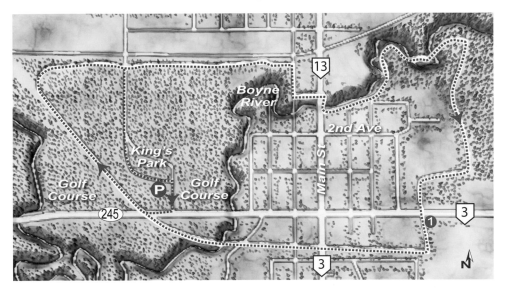

his views on temperance and women's suffrage. Her theatrical production of 'Votes for Men' brilliantly parodied his pomposity and patronizing manner and helped bring about his political downfall. This ridicule and scandal have obscured some of his many achievements. Many believe that we have the Roblin family to thank for presiding over the transformation of our province from a pioneer society into a modern capitalist economy.

distance

5.5 km loop

Pick up a map / brochure at Tourist Info Centre located at Syl's Drive Inn ❶ off Hwy 3

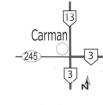

what's special

The rugged beauty of Precambrian Shield is all around you on this route. Highlights include a white birch forest along the rocky Heritage Channel Walk and the spectacular Pinawa Suspension Bridge, a 50 metre foot bridge spanning the Pinawa Channel.

distance

10 km loop

some history

The Pinawa Channel was blasted out in the early 1900s to provide a reliable water supply to the hydro-electric plant at Pinawa Falls. That plant was decommissioned in 1951 and today the channel functions mainly as an excellent canoe route. At the end of the channel, you'll cross a diversion dam, walk a short distance up Highway 211 and into the town of Pinawa.

This town has the feel of a well-manicured suburb somehow stranded in the wilds of the Canadian Shield. Pinawa was built in the 1960s to house the employees of western Canada's only nuclear research centre and was intricately planned to be a model community. The townsite on a widening of the Winnipeg River was chosen for its visual appeal. It had beautiful rolling terrain and a lake for a backyard. Pinawa was designed as a well-treed, well-scrubbed, suburban-style enclave.

All went according to plan until downsizing hit this one-industry town and put its prosperity at risk. Government cutbacks started in 1988, and today the Atomic Energy laboratories are essentially out of commission. Nevertheless, the townsfolk are still upbeat and have great optimism for the future. New industry will no doubt find this place irresistible with its picturesque resort location and excellent facilities. As well, the stock of affordable homes make the town an attractive retirement haven. This is a true paradise for the nature lover and sports enthusiast. Fishing, canoeing, hiking, skiing, golf, tennis, and swimming are right outside your door.

Ironwood Trail

This interpretive self-guiding nature trail is named for the ironwood trees found along it. These trees are at the most northern edge of their range and are therefore a rarity in Manitoba.

Heritage Channel Trail

4

5

Pinawa Channel

3

2

211

what you'll find

This entire route is signed with Trans Canada Trail markers with the exception of the stretch from ❺ the suspension bridge south to ❻ the TCT turn-off.

Pinawa

6

P

1

Ironwood Trail

Winnipeg River

N

🅿	Park & begin hike at the marina in the centre of town
❶	marina
❷	swimming beach
❸	golf course
❹	diversion dam
❺	suspension foot bridge
❻	Trans Canada Trail turn-off

distance

8.5 km loop

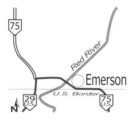

what you'll find

Our route takes you out & back along the banks of the Red River under a canopy of giant elms & cottonwoods to historic Fort Dufferin, then circles through town.

some history

From the outset, Emerson was destined for great things. It was a boom town - a rival to Winnipeg. Steamships travelled up from the States, trains arrived daily, and settlers poured through town on their way to southern Manitoba. Manufacturing flourished, elaborate public buildings were erected, and by 1883 Emerson's population numbered 10,000. Its destiny as a great metropolis seemed assured, but the town was staking its future on a rail line. In those days, the railway ruled the political and physical lives of communities and many a town found their bright hopes dashed when the rail lines passed them by. Emerson's bid for the CPR transcontinental line turned out to be a reckless and costly gamble. It lost the line and the town went bankrupt.

Evidence of 'boom town' Emerson remains to this day. There are several private residences from that grand era still standing - Bryce House at 99 Assiniboine, Fairbanks Mansion at the corner of 3rd & Rouseau and Kelvinside (Aunt Maude's Tea Room) at 57 - 4th St. The elaborate public buildings from Emerson's boom period were however lost to fire or flooding. The present Town Hall / Court House was erected in 1917. It is now a provincial heritage building. The 1870 log Customs House, the first in western Canada, still stands at the edge of town.

Fort Dufferin, two miles north of Emerson,

was marked by laziness, recklessness and heavy drinking, and one can only imagine the citizenry of Emerson as unimpressed with him as he with their town. Fort Dufferin's final role was as an immigration depot when the wave of Mennonite settlers embarked to take up their homesteads.

yearly flooding

From the beginning, Emerson has been plagued with floods. There is much evidence of years of high water along the Fort Dufferin trail with old elms & cottonwoods dying off from prolonged immersion. Emerson's first major flood was in 1882 when the waters rose to such a height that a steamship sailed right up the main street to unload its cargo. After the disastrous flood in 1950 when the town was evacuated, a ring dike was built and Emerson took on the feel of a walled city. This dike served them well in 1975 but in 1997's 'flood of the century' two more feet needed to be added to the top. As you walk along the top of the dike, think of the mighty Red River a scant 24 inches beneath your feet.

was built by the Canadian Boundary Commission in 1872 and was later home to the North West Mounted Police. The NWMP used the fort in the spring of 1874 as the marshalling area for their great 'March West' to bring law & order to the Canadian West. They used it again in the winter of 1874-5 as the headquarters of 'D' Division. One officer of 'Company D' was a Frank Dickens, third son of writer Charles. Frank wrote many letters home to England describing his impressions of Canada. Of Fort Dufferin, he wrote, "This climatically petrified post is positioned precisely on the planet to be the only place in the world where a person warms of the prospect of being sent to H--l!" Frank's unspectacular career

P	Park & begin hike at the community park adjacent to the railbridge
1	footbridge attached to the railbridge
2	Fort Dufferin site & self-guiding interpretive trails
3	town ring dike

MINNEDOSA

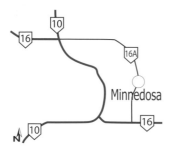

This town is beautifully situated. It has tree-lined streets dotted with old stone buildings and the Little Saskatchewan River snaking through its centre.

Hwy 262 marks the spot where Tanner's bridge once spanned the river.

Across the road at the bottom of Cemetery Hill, you'll find 'In the Wind Manor'. Built in 1892 by stone mason James McKay, this heritage home is a fine example of Scottish stone cutting. Still visible in the front yard are the oxcart tracks of the old Carlton Trail.

The exploits of John Tanner's grandfather, 'Falcon' Tanner, have been immortalized in several books including 'Black Falcon' written in 1954 by Olive Knox and illustrated by Clarence Tillenius. Falcon was eight years old in 1789 when he was abducted by the Shawnees. A wise and gentle woman

distance

6.5 km loop

some history

Minnedosa owes its establishment to the Tanner family - a colourful clan whose history in our province dates back to the 1700s. John and Catherine Tanner moved to this strategic site in 1869 hoping to make a dollar or two off the great tide of settlers passing through on the Carlton Trail. They set up a toll bridge on the Little Saskatchewan River and built a 'stopping house' and post office. For decades the Carlton Trail was the most heavily used settlement route in western Canada and Tanner's Crossing attracted hundreds of pioneers and fur traders as they made their way west.

John and Catherine were both 3rd generation Metis. As was often the case, they were made to feel unwelcome when white settlers moved in. Tanner's Crossing Village had attracted the attention of Joseph Armitage, a miller from Ontario. He persuaded the Tanners to sell their land for $50. Soon after, Armitage had the site surveyed into lots and renamed Minnedosa. A cairn in Centennial Park on Beach Rd/

P	Park at the Cenotaph off Main St and find the community pathway that runs under the railway bridge
1	Bison Park
2	Centennial Park heritage site & 'In the Wind Manor' house
3	Minnedosa cemetery
4	public beach
5	Flag Walk
6	Heritage Village
7	Castle Bed & Breakfast

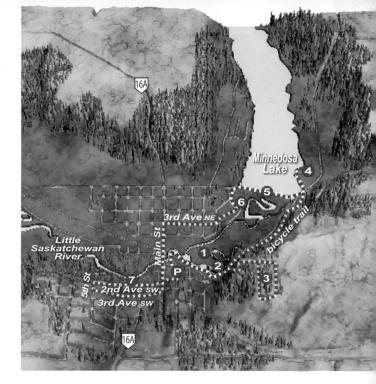

chief of the Ottawas, who had lost a son, later adopted him. He was taught to hunt, fish, paddle and build canoes, ride horses, and fight his foster family's enemies. Falcon became an excellent hunter and trapper and through the years became intimately familiar with Ontario and Manitoba forts and waterways. By 1816, he was guiding Lord Selkirk soldiers from Fort William to the Red River settlement.

distance

15 km loop

Pick up an interpretative trail guide at the Heritage North Museum, the train station or City Hall.

what you'll find

The City of Thompson Millennium Trail is a 15 km hike and bike loop around the city. The crushed rock trail is open year round to non-motorized travel. Walking, hiking and mountain biking are popular in the summer while walking and cross country skiing are winter favourites. With sections winding through pristine boreal forest and making use of some of the city's sidewalks and walking paths, the Millennium Trail shows off the best that Thompson has to offer. Along the route you'll see the King Miner Statue,

Calypso Orchids

P	Find & park at city hall off Mystery Lake Road
1	Find the 'Bailey' bridge & pick up the trail
2	granite cliffs & Rotary Outlook
3	Heritage North Museum
4	Find Calypso orchids at edge of forest trail (in early June)

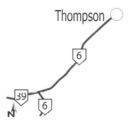

some history

The Millenium Trail was built in 2000 & 2001. It was designed to give residents an attractive, easily accessed hiking and bicycling trail and also to attract and hold tourists, especially the many that pass through en route to Churchill. (The trail passes close by the train station.)

Heritage North Museum, MacLean Park, Norplex Pool, Waterski Club, Recreation Centre and the Thompson Zoo.

Beginning at the Zoo is a one kilometre self guided Interpretative Trail. Using a descriptive brochure and trail markers one can see unique features of flora, fauna and northern terrain.

Bailey bridge

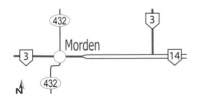

distance

10 km one way / 20 km out & back

We recommend you cache a car at the Morden Research Centre & hike one way only

some history

Morden is a prosperous, pretty and well-treed town. Tucked into the escarpment and sitting beneath the protective Pembina Hills, this area can claim a significantly longer growing season than is general on the Canadian prairies. Its low altitude, coupled with dark loamy soil, make it favourable for growing hot-weather and long season crops, and allow it to claim the title "Garden Spot" of Manitoba. For these reasons the federal Department of Agriculture decided in 1914 to establish an experimental station here to take advantage of these favourable conditions. Its first purpose was to assist homemakers with their orchards and gardens but it

what's special

Scenic highlights include a climb down the steep valley walls of Dead Horse Creek, the new footpath along Lake Minnewasta's shoreline, a descent from the Manitoba Escarpment onto a community pathway through the golf course & Morden's beautiful collection of heritage buildings.

went on to explore a range of field crops, such as corn for grain and sunflowers for oil, that might be profitably adapted to the western part of the Red River Valley. Many varieties of flax, sunflowers, buckwheat, field pea and field corn developed at Morden have become industry standards in both domestic and international markets. The Morden Research Centre of today also specializes in developing landscape plants for the prairies and maintains 'germplasm' (genetic blueprints) for winter-hardy woody ornamentals, fruit, and special crops, as part of a national genetic resource conservation program. Aside from research, the Centre offers a scenic retreat for picnics or a leisurely walk through the various plantations with a 50 acre arboretum of an astonishingly diverse range of native and exotic woody plants.

One of the town's greatest assets is its large stock of heritage buildings designed with quality and extravagance and now used as

P	Park at Trans Canada Trail sign on municipal road 11W, 2 miles west of Hwy 432
1	Cross Dead Horse Creek & turn right / east at top of hill
2	Colert Beach
3	community pathway through golf course
4	Walk up to Mountain St / Hwy 432 & turn left, then north to Stephen & turn right
5	Morden Research Centre

both residences and business establishments. These buildings offer a fascinating array of styles and building materials, and those constructed of indigenous stone hold a special attraction and the aura of romance.

Walking along Stephen St. you'll pass four of the finest stone houses on the Central Plains. There are also some unique public buildings - gems like the old Post Office (corner of Stephen & 8th St.)

Many walkers may decide that the high point of their Morden tour is the Kinsmen Community Footpath through the Minnewasta Golf Course. It is difficult to overstate the significance of having a walking trail through this beautiful golf course which straddles the steep rise of the escarpment. As a rule, golf courses, public and private alike, obstruct pedestrian access to their grounds and in doing so deprive great numbers of disgruntled walkers of the opportunity to enjoy some of the most scenic spots in the country. The Kinsmen club and citizens of Morden have done something very special and very progressive here. They

deserve high praise for sharing their beautiful corner of the world with everyone and we can only hope this community footpath will become a model for the rest of Manitoba.

some history

Since the beginning of human history on our continent, the site of Portage la Prairie has been a strategic location in Canada. Its name and history go back to French explorer LaVerendrye who established his fort two miles from the present city in 1738. First Portage la Prairie was important for exploration and fur trade and later it was a magnet for early settlement. Metis farmers from the overcrowded Red River Settlement were the first farmers here. Later in the century they were largely shunted aside by settlers from Ontario and Britain who made a beeline for the rich farmland. With the interest and enthusiasm of Ontarians & British, it is not surprising that by 1880, when the railway reached Portage, most of the Portage Plains were settled. Within a few years the area was producing a grade of wheat unsurpassed on the world market. Sitting in the heart of the fertile Portage Plains, this is the richest farming belt in Manitoba.

One early British settler, Robert B. Hill, went on to become a 'mover and shaker' whose influence continues to this day. Hill was

highlights

This walk gives you the opportunity to really appreciate the scenery around Crescent Lake and Island Park. Beginning with a walk through the arboretum on Island Park, our route takes you out around the Lake, through the pleasant residential area of Koko Platz, out to a new portion of community pathway, then up into the business district to check out some heritage buildings.

P	Intersedtion of Brandon Ave & Massey Cres
1	Crescent Lake walking path
2	Enter community pathway
3	City Hall
4	Arboretum

a blacksmith and carriage maker by trade. He came to be recognized as Portage la Prairie's first historian and a preeminent authority on Manitoba's early settlement. In his books, he amused readers with his 'behind the scenes' tale of Portage la Prairie's experiment as a republic. Of more importance to us today is the outcome of his influcnce to create Crescent Lake & Island Park.

The Assiniboine River had created an oxbow which most people saw as 'just a slough'. The ever creative Hill sparked citizens' imagination about what the area could become when he began renting row boats in the summer of 1892 (He probably built them too). This boating 'on the slough' became very popular with the young people. Up untll that time, the island was considered a primitive section of town. By 1896 there were park and exhibition grounds and a turf club. Later, water was pumped in from the Assiniboine to raise the level of the lake, and a bridge was built. The semi circular lake then effectively created the 'Island'. A history of 'Island Park' tells us that Hill himself was out plowing and harrowing the soil in readiness for sodding and seeding the public park.

Island Park is now the centrepiece of the city. A four acre arboretum has a collection of prairie hardy trees, shrubs and vines. Descendants of R B Hill live on Island Park to this day, operating the large and prosperous Mayfair Farm and one of the prettiest u-pick strawberry patches in the province.

distance

8 km loop

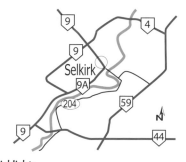

highlights

The Red River is the heart and soul of this community and Selkirk's maritime heritage is much in evidence on our route. You'll pass by the Slough, Manitoba's largest inland port, and a fine display of former lake vessels at the Selkirk Marine Museum - all prime attractions. As well, you'll follow park trails through towering river bottom forest and walk quiet tree-lined streets past the homes of Selkirk's earliest citizens.

some history

Political decisions have, throughout the ages, denied Selkirk its rightful place of pre-eminence in Manitoba. It was certainly blessed with the most advantageous site for a community on the Red River, with high banks that defend its residents against even the most devastating floods. It had two excellent natural harbours, rich farmlands surrounding and deep water navigation to Lake Winnipeg's natural resources and the Hudson's Bay route.

In the 1870s, Selkirk was about to become the Inter-Ocean Centre of Canada. It just needed the transcontinental rail line to come through where speculated. A furious battle raged over whether the railway bridge should be built at Selkirk, as originally anticipated, or at Winnipeg, as the Minister of Railways seemed to favour. Of course, the Winnipeg newspapers and its residents clamoured for the southern crossing but Sir Sandford Fleming, CPR's chief engineer, strongly favoured Selkirk. In the end, government ministers overruled engineers and Winnipeg, that muddy, low-lying, flood prone settlement, was awarded the line. The dubious motives

annual 'Highland Gathering' in Selkirk Park

fishing on the pier

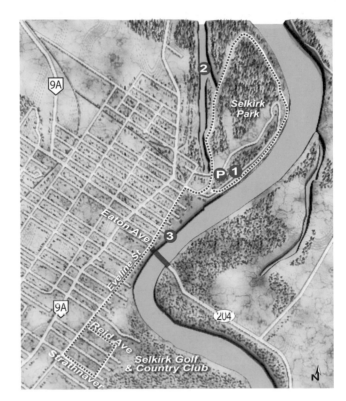

🅿	Park at Marine Museum
❶	Selkirk Community Trail
❷	West Slough
❸	Selkirk pier

behind that decision cause some resentment to this day.

It's a story told by many towns in Manitoba. The rail line passes them by and their bright and shining future goes with it. For all that, Selkirk went on to enjoy considerable prosperity although on a smaller scale and it continued to promote itself as having the most advantageous and picturesque situation in the province.

Selkirk's most important geographical feature is the West Slough, a naturally deep and sheltered inlet. Hudson Bay Company records show that it was used by them to safely winter their York boats and later it attracted the attention of railway surveyors and lumber and fishing companies requiring safe harbour for their fleets. In 1913, the local newspaper announced - "No other place along the Red River could afford boats the security of winter shelter that the famous West Slough could. Selkirk will always continue to be part of Canada's great inland waterways." He was right. Today, many

large river excursion boats are still wintered here and the Canadian Coast Guard maintains a sizeable facility for its dredgers and patrol vessels.

Fittingly, Selkirk Park is now home to a wonderful marine museum. It includes a simulated underwater diving display, an authentic lighthouse from Black Bear Island, marine artifacts, a display of local fish, and a terrific collection of famous lake boats such as the 1897 S.S. Kenora

and the 1915 ice breaker C.B.S. Bradbury.

250

2

Souris

22

N

distance

6 km loop

what's special

Souris takes the prize for the prettiest main street in Manitoba. Set in the picturesque Souris River Valley, this town has a lot to attract tourists and walkers alike.

some history

This town owes its existence to a colourful character by the name of Squire Sowden. The Squire had spent a lot of time exploring half of western Canada before deciding on this site as ideal for his ambitious plans. His aim was to establish a new elite community - a select group of landed gentry that would tame the prairie frontier. He brought his first party of hand-picked settlers out in 1881. They were well-to-do Ontarians and apparently had sufficient breeding to fit the Squire's requirements. By the turn of the century, Souris society was setting the tone for refinement on the prairies. The hills echoed with the horns and hounds of fox hunting by day and the declamations of touring dramatic groups by night. The luxury of the Souris Opera House was a match for many in Europe and cricket, polo and tennis were the games of choice. Sowden established the first Souris brickyard and built a number of fine commercial buildings including the opera house which he named Sowden Hall. He built a large mansion for himself and in 1904, the famous swinging bridge. As the owner of 7000 acres adjacent to the town site, he was anxious to develop a new residential area on the east side of town and needed this convenient foot passage to connect the new development.

On your route, you'll encounter many reminders of Squire Sowden's influence and benevolence. We begin the walk in Victoria Park which is on land donated to the town by Sowden in 1897 to commemorate Queen Victoria's Jubilee. The swinging bridge, of course, was initially built by

the Squire although it was replaced in 1976 after the original was destroyed by raging flood water. (This new bridge is 177 metres long - the longest suspension bridge in Canada). As you look west from the bridge, you can't fail to notice what looks like a castle. This imposing two

storey mansion was built by Sowden's son Fred in 1910 and now houses the Hillcrest Museum.

In the centre of town, Crescent Avenue is perched high atop a steep bank overlooking Plum Creek and Victoria Park. This is the town's focal point and a treasure trove of fine Victorian brick buildings.

P	*Park in the centre of Victoria Park & find nature trail up the bank to the south*
1	*historic oak tree*
2	*lookout tower*
3	*gazebo*
4	*swinging bridge*

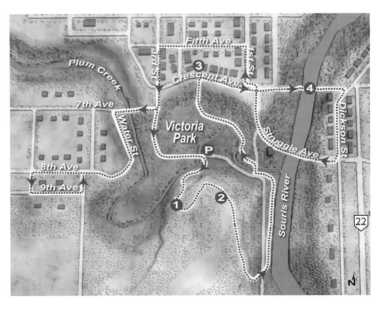

distance

11 km loop

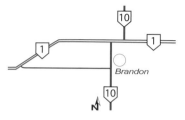

what's special

Brandon is a great city for walkers and our route follows sidewalks as well as some wonderful community pathways. Highlights are the beautiful Eleanor Kidd Park plus a downtown tour past some of the city's finest heritage buildings.

some history

In 1881 Brandon was transformed overnight from a sparse collection of settlers in the middle of a prairie wilderness to a full fledged city. General Rosser of the Canadian Pacific Railway selected this site as a division point on the new rail line and summoned into being a transportation and trading centre that exploded into a population of thousands in the space of a year.

Nellie McClung in her book 'Clearing the West', writes about visiting the city as a girl in 1883. She describes the ubiquitous clash and clatter of construction. "The predominant smell was of lumber; shingles and tar paper and from the time we entered the city, we could hear sounds of building, hammering and sawing .." She also relates her wonder

at catching sight of "the great yellow brick court house, the largest building I had ever seen."

Another building that may have caught McClung's eye is the brick cottage of Clifford Sifton at 113 Princess. As a young lawyer in the 1880s, Sifton saw the economic promise of his adopted home more clearly than most. He was a man of great ambition both for himself and his country. He launched a

foot bridge over the Assiniboine

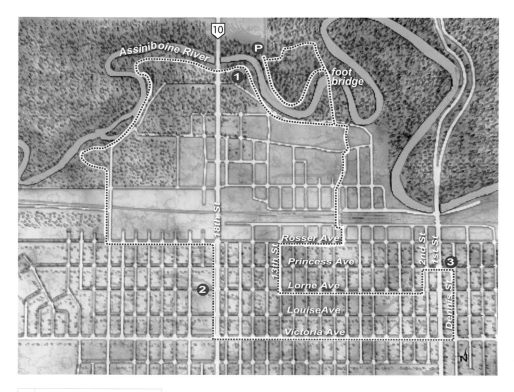

	Riverbank Discovery Centre
❶	Eleanor Kidd Park
❷	Brandon University
❸	Sifton House

successful political career as befit a man of ambition and went on to become the federal Minister of the Interior. In that post, he embarked on "the greatest promotion campaign which Canada or the world, had ever known". It was a campaign born out of an aggressive immigration policy and saw more than a million eastern Europeans leave their homeland to settle Canada's prairie provinces. It is hard to overstate the impact that this man had on the development and prosperity of western Canada. Sifton's most lasting monument is the rich and varied population he encouraged to settle our province.

distance

Brandon has a wonderful collection of heritage buildings. A walking tour guide, which describes the architectural history of the city, is available from the Riverbank Discovery Centre

Sifton cottage at 113 Princess Ave

Fort Dauphin Museum

distance

6 km loop

	Vermillion Park
❶	CN Station / Chamber of Commerce
❷	Ukrainian Catholic Church of the Resurrection
❸	Fort Dauphin Museum

some history

During the early 1880s the first settlers arrived from Ontario and the British Isles and established Old Dauphin. With the coming of the railway these settlers moved the town lock stock and barrel two miles south to the current location. These early pioneers dominated the political, cultural and economic life

Ukrainian Catholic Church of the Resurrection

of the town for the first quarter century but by the 1920s Dauphin was changing. After the first world war, Ukrainian settlers who had initially homesteaded the surrounding farmlands and wooded area near Riding Mountain, started finding jobs in town, many with the railway. Soon they became the predominant ethnic group and today, Dauphin is considered the Ukrainian capital of Manitoba, most famous for Canada's National Ukrainian Festival, held every summer.

what you'll find

Our tour begins with the nature trail loop through Vermillion Park, then heads to the CN station / chamber of commerce where you can pick up an architectural walking tour guide. This brochure is beautifully illustrated and includes an outline of the town's history.

One of the most eye-catching buildings along our route is the Ukrainian Catholic Church of the Resurrection. With its multidomed silhouette, brilliant paintings and rich icons, it brings a breath of the exotic Byzantine empire to the Manitoba prairie. A tour of the interior can be arranged by phoning 204.638-5511.

The Fort Dauphin Museum lends an insight into the lives and history of the early settlers and the native inhabitants before them. Exhibits include a blacksmith shop, a fur trading post, and a trapper's house. The museum also displays many native artifacts and houses an archaeological laboratory.

what's special

Our route takes you through one of Manitoba's oldest and possibly its finest cottage development.

Those original ideals still protect the area from thoughtless change. Improvements such as electricity were cautiously weighed against the loss of trees along the back lanes before being approved. Vehicular traffic is still banned and the shady lanes that connect the cottages to the parking lot and other amenities such as tennis courts, bakery and library, have become attractions in and of themselves. These lanes provide miles of safe and scenic pathways for cyclists and walkers.

some history

Walking into Victoria Beach is like entering an elegant preserve from another era. The original developers deserve credit for this. In 1913, a group of private investors formed the Victoria Beach Investment Company. No flashy dance halls or amusement parks for this group. It was their intention to create an exclusive oasis for their families and friends. They drew up a slew of bylaws and caveats that ensured trees were protected and cabins tastefully designed. Automobiles were banned and any commercial development that might attract the 'day-trippers' was severely circumscribed. If some of the restrictions seem repressive by today's standards, the end result is an undeniably attractive summer resort.

distance

6 km loop

You'll find some of the oldest and most interesting cottages in the province, some of them built from tamarack logs brought down from the top of Lake Winnipeg. Along each lane you notice the lush variety of native plants and beautifully kept gardens, no doubt the result of many years of annual Victoria Beach Garden Competitions.

FYI

What sets Victoria Beach apart from other cottage resorts is its 'no car' rule. From May through Sept, all residents and visitors park in the same parking lot at the edge of the resort. From here they take a taxi, cycle or walk.

P	*Park in the community parking lot at entrance to resort*
1	*Victoria Beach clubhouse*
2	*town centre*
3	*Patricia Beach*
4	*King Edward Beach*

CENTENNIAL TRAIL

distanc

11.4 km one way / 22.8 km out & back
We recommend you cache a car at one end & hike one way only

some history

The Centennial Trail covers some of the most beautiful terrain in the Whiteshell and is marked by a series of cairns - rather like a treasure hunt. You won't find it on your park map. The trail was originally developed by a group of boy scouts.

Back in 1970, Scout leader, Vern Dutton, decided that building a hiking trail would be a terrific project for the Pembina District Scouts and a wonderful way to celebrate Manitoba's Centennial. For years, Dutton organized an annual pilgrimage to the trail, where the scouts worked at adding stones to the cairn markers and nailing up wooden plaques with their distinctive Scout emblem. To this day, the Scouts and Girl Guides of Canada continue to maintain, improve and expand the trail as a 'good deed' / community service.

One other individual needs to be singled out for her efforts. In the early 1990s, stewardship of this project was passed on to Guide leader Cindy Bell and it is very much through her good works that we are now all able to enjoy the full 11 km stretch of trail.

what's special

The trail begins across the highway from the Bear Lake Trail Wayside Park. You'll need to scramble up the rock ledge to find the first cairn marker. (You'll also find Trans Canada Trail markers along the route.) About 800 metres into the hike you'll cross a stream on top of a beaver dam. Depending on the water level, this may or may not be a simple matter. Caution is advised.

49°49'55.0"N, 95°19'44.5"W	**P** *Bear Lake Picnic site*
49°49'36.7"N, 95°19'36.3"W	**1** *beaver dam crossiing*
49°48'53.5"N, 95°16'52.5"W	**2** *Turtle's Back exit*

49°48'55.3"N, 95°15'23.6"W	**3** *emergency exit*
49°48'32.1"N, 95°14'22.8"W	**4** *McGillivray Falls*

Christel Bischoff

what's special

This is a trail for nimble hikers. There are some steep grades, and at certain points, rock scrambling is required. The trail follows a series of granite ridges and part of its charm is the contrast between these long stretches of bare rock and the lush surrounding forest. You'll trek up and along rock spines, then down onto thick cushions of moss through the quiet stillness of a bog. The sound of rushing water announces the end of the trail at pretty McGillivray Falls.

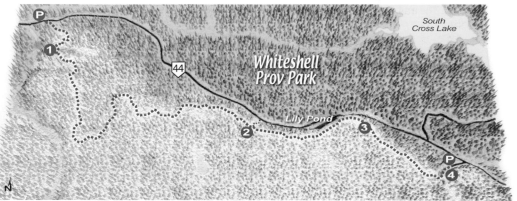

South Cross Lake

Whiteshell Prov Park

Lily Pond

what's special

With one spectacular view after another, hiking this popular trail is the very best way to appreciate the beauty of Clear Lake.

Riding Mountain
Nat'l Park
10
Clear Lake
North Trail
19
N

some history

Clear Lake is the jewel in the middle of Riding Mountain. It was the crystal clear beauty of this lake that first prompted Manitobans to lobby for the establishment of a national park in 1930.

From the outset, Riding Mountain was considered a premier summer playground and most of it was designated as "wilderness". This hike takes you past the only built-up areas in this large park. A small section around the south and north east end of the lake was developed into the popular townsite of Wasagaming, the prestigious cottages along the south shore and an additional subdivision along the north shore. The park's primary focus is 'conservation and wilderness'. Any plans for further development take a "status quo" approach of containment.

distance

12.5 km one way / 25 km out & back

We recommend you cache a car at one end & hike one way only

how to get there

Our route follows the north shore trail of Clear Lake from Spruces Picnic site running east past the north shore cottage development, the Glen Beag picnic area, the golf course, and then back to Wasagaming on the Lakeshore Walk.

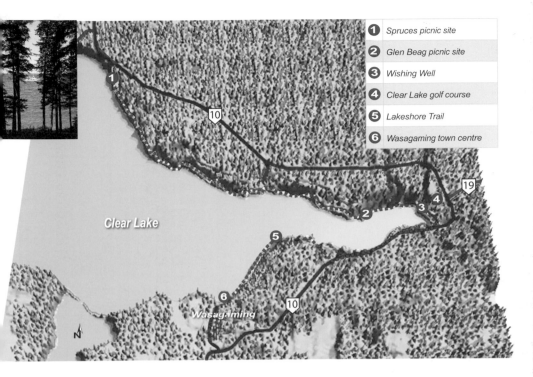

1 Spruces picnic site
2 Glen Beag picnic site
3 Wishing Well
4 Clear Lake golf course
5 Lakeshore Trail
6 Wasagaming town centre

Clear Lake

Wasagaming

Whiteshell Prov Park

Mantario Trail

307
309
307
44
44
1

some history

Developed by the Manitoba Naturalists Society in 1978, the Mantario Trail showcases our provinces's first designated wilderness zone and a part of Manitoba's Precambrian Shield that is characterized by rugged granite ridges, deep clear lakes and lush forests.

From Castle Rock, you take in a panoramic view that includes Camp Alloway across the lake. The camp is named for leading citizen William Alloway. In a province that has more than its share of famous philanthropists, Bill Alloway deserves a place of special distinction. He first arrived here in 1870 as an 18 year old private with the Ontario Rifles who were here to put down the alleged insurrection at Red River. Alloway saw his future in Winnipeg and put down roots. With a decidedly nonchalant approach to his career path, he took a job as a policeman, then opened a tobacco shop while trying his hand as an amateur veterinarian. Later he launched a transportation business, and at one point owned a fleet of six thousand Red River carts and oxen teams. By the time he was thrity-five, he had co-founded one of the largest financial houses in western Canada and had made pots of money. When he died in 1930, he left his entire fortune of more than two million dollars (a phenomenal sum for its time) to charity - the Winnipeg Foundation. It seems fitting that his wonderful generosity should be recognized by giving his name to such a beautiful place as Camp Alloway.

what's special

This day hike into Castle Rock is the most northerly section of the Mantario Trail and gives you a taste of Manitoba's premier wilderness hiking. The Mantario attracts hikers from all over the world and covers exceptional terrain in a magnificent setting.

distance

7 km one way / 14 km out & back

P Mantario trailhead sign

1 portage trail to Crowduck Lake

2 campsite

3 Trail up to Castle Rock

Big Whiteshell Lake

Post Island

Castle Rock

N

caution

The marker that directs you to Castle Rock is makeshift and not that easy to see. In places the trail may be overgrown and difficult to follow. Other challenges may include wet, slippery rocks, beaver dams and scrambles up high rock ridges.

what you'll find

This is a remarkable example of what volunteer trail builders can accomplish. The Stanley Trail Group designed their portion of the Trans Canada Trail to showcase the scenic Manitoba Escarpment. The route winds through terrain that varies from flat farm field to steep hill and follows public roads as well as some excellent new trail through pasture and woods on private land. One particularly scenic stretch follows a creek bed down the escarpment.

We recommend beginning at the north end (You'll spot a MTS building off Hwy 432) and caching a car at south end of the route. You'll find a parking lot and Trans Canada Trail kiosk at both ends of this hike. Long stretches are on quiet dirt roads but there is a one mile section in the middle of this route that's on a high gravel road where busy truck traffic can be a concern.

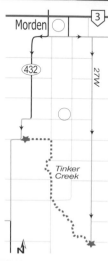

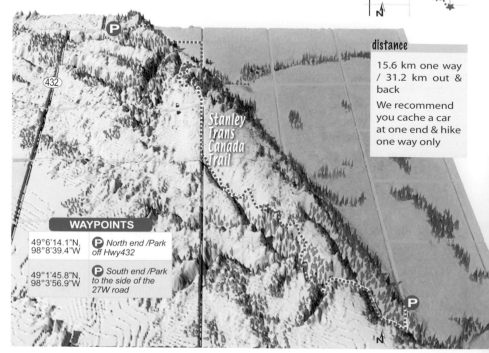

distance

15.6 km one way / 31.2 km out & back

We recommend you cache a car at one end & hike one way only

Stanley Trans Canada Trail

WAYPOINTS

49°6'14.1"N, 98°8'39.4"W	**P** North end /Park off Hwy432
49°1'45.8"N, 98°3'56.9"W	**P** South end /Park to the side of the 27W road

how to get there

The western trailhead for this route can be found east off Hwy 5 and directly across from the road to the Spruce Woods campground office - where parking is available.

To find the eastern trailhead turn north off Hwy 2 onto Park Road (which is just a half mile east of the town of Cypress River). Drive approx 8 km. You'll find a trail intersecting the road and a Trans Canada Trail sign.

distance

15.6 km one way / 31.2 km out & back

We recommend you cache a car at one end & hike one way only

what you'll find

This route is part of the Trans Canada Trail and it highlights the diversity of this picturesque park. Beginning at the west end, this hike runs along the high banks of the Assiniboine River - past Steel's Ferry Overlook then on a sandy cart track through rolling grassy plains and evergreen forest ending at Park Road. The trail is well marked with signs every .5 km.

Frits Stevens

how to get there

Find this trail off PR 307 between the Bannock Point petroforms and Pine Point Rapids trails. The turnoff has a stop sign and is marked ER31.

This is a wilderness backcountry hike and it's easy to get disoriented. To ensure your safety you should carry a GPS device.

Whiteshell
Prov Park

307

Trail to
George
Lake

309

307

44

44

1

N

distance

11.5 km one way / 23 km out & back

This is the most challenging day hike we have in the book. You need to be an experienced hiker to trek it in one day. We recommend it for backpackers. If the trail is wet, allow at least 9 hours for the hike.

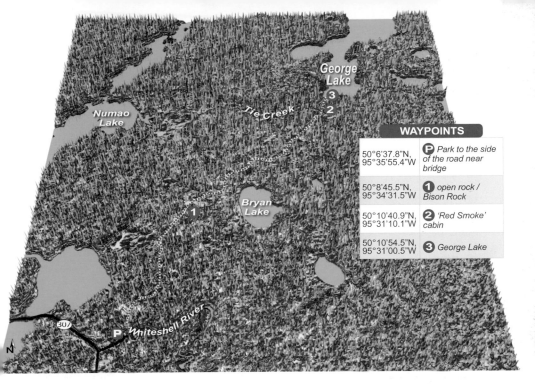

George Lake

Numao Lake

Tie Creek

Bryan Lake

1

2

3

Whiteshell River

P

307

	WAYPOINTS
50°6'37.8"N, 95°35'55.4"W	**P** Park to the side of the road near bridge
50°8'45.5"N, 95°34'31.5"W	**1** open rock / Bison Rock
50°10'40.9"N, 95°31'10.1"W	**2** 'Red Smoke' cabin
50°10'54.5"N, 95°31'00.5"W	**3** George Lake

some history

George Lake is an isolated wilderness accessed only by ATV or on foot. It's famous for its rugged beauty, its water clarity and its excellent fishing. It has the distinction of holding the Manitoba weight record for Walleye and is particularly famous for its trophy Smallmouth Bass and Lake Trout.

Most people get into the lake from the north, boating down from Point du Bois on the Winnipeg River, then taking a one mile portage. Our route goes in from the south taking an old cart track that early settlers followed to their homesteads. Although, how anyone farmed in here defies imagination.

what you'll find

The track, now used by ATVs or 'quads', is not an official park trail. There are no trail markers, but it winds through a particularly scenic area. The beginning and end sections of the route take us through lush forest of spruce and birch. Expect some muddy areas and makeshift bridges. In the middle we get out onto broad expanses of rock - the classic rugged beauty of the Precambrian Shield. The destination for this hike is the backcountry campsite on the pristine rock shoreline of George Lake.

When Cotton came out, he shrewdly decided to lease land instead of purchasing. The terms offered a rare opportunity for a skilled farmer - $2 a year for a section of land. The land owner had a fair bargain as well because he would keep possession of all improvements to his property after 5 years. Cotton prospered with the help of his four strong sons and continued to expand his leasehold. By 1898, he had accumulated an astonishing $30,000 in profits. Now he was ready to put down roots and secure his sons' inheritance. But he wasn't going to pay the inflated land prices of the Tiger Hills. He had his eye on the much touted Swan River

some history

This part of the Tiger Hills saw a large scale movement of transplanted Ontarians mixed with a sprinkling of immigrants from Great Britain pour in during the 1870s & 1880s. These people quickly came to dominate and transform the local community. The original Metis settlers were pushed to one side and a predominantly WASP society was established.

These new settlers have been referred to as 'privileged settlers'. They were, by and large men with a fair amount of capital and often as great an interest in land speculation as in farming. They were also practical farmers with a high degree of agricultural experience and expertise.

One early settler who is representative of this group is A J Cotton. He wrote a detailed journal that gives us insight into the times.

Valley where rumour had it that the land was prime and the price was cheap. Cotton had to see for himself. For him the rich loamy soil of Treherne was the 'gold standard'. He hitched a team to a covered wagon, loaded on a basket of Treherne soil and headed up the Pelly Trail. If the Swan River Valley could match Tiger Hills dirt, he would finally plunk down his money and become a landowner.

Cotton was the exception. Most settlers remained in the Tiger Hills for generations, as evidenced by the number of 'Century Farms' in this fertile and picturesque part of Manitoba.

distance

18 km loop

what's special

The Tiger Hills are a western extension of the Pembina Hills and offer up some terrific views of the rolling prairie in the valley below. Our route runs on mile roads up into the hills through bluffs of oak and Manitoba maple; past roadside wild fruit & flowers and gently rolling grain fields.

P	Park at the community centre on Van Zile St.
1	cut bank & recycle depot
2	communications tower

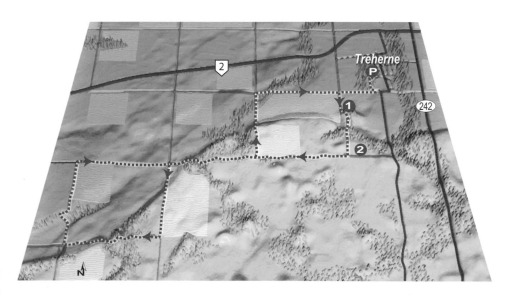

what you'll find

This trail is not an easy one. It is marked by cairns but not an overabundance of them.

So you need to keep a sharp eye on the markers. The rocky path can be slippery and there are some fairly steep climbs up high rock ridges. As well, at certain times of the year, the boardwalks at the west end of the pathway may be underwater. The rewards of this hike however are undeniable.

Adding to the pleasure of the walk is the rich variety of plant life. Wildflowers and thick carpets of moss are everywhere.

The trail ends at the mouth of Black River where you'll find a pretty set of rapids. At this point you're just a short hike from Hwy 314. You may want to make arrangements to use two cars and do the hike just one way.

distance

8 km one way / 16 km out & back

Pick up the Black Lake campground map at the park office. It has directions to the trail head.

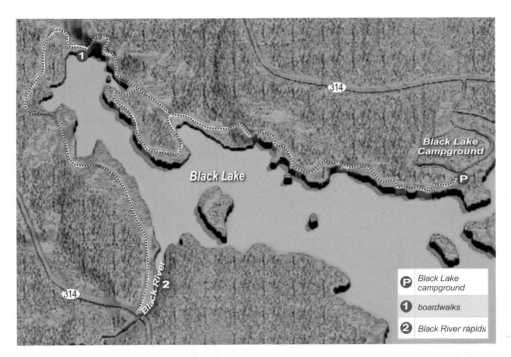

Black Lake

Black Lake Campground

314

P

1

2 Black River

314

P	Black Lake campground
1	boardwalks
2	Black River rapids

314

ONTARIO

Black Lake Trail

Nopiming Prov Park

315

what's special

This craggy rock-hewn landscape with towering stands of spruce and jack pine can be breathtaking in its beauty. The trail closely follows the rocky Black Lake shoreline. It is an up and down path with some magnificent viewpoints.

Turtle Mountain
Prov Park   James
              Lake Trail
N
    U.S. Border

distance

15 km loop

Pick up the Turtle Mountain Park map at the park office. It has directions to the trail head.

what you'll find

The James Lake loop trailhead is found at the west end of the Adam Lake campground. This 15 km route, marked in orange, takes you out around James Lake and provides a nice overview of the park. The trail, once a lumber road, is now a wide grassy track that winds through rolling hills and crosses numerous creeks. There's a lovely view from the cabin at James Lake. This is a good spot to stop for lunch.

Near the end of the route you pass a swimming beach and walk over a causeway. The loop is well marked to the causeway but after that there are several intersecting trails on the way back to the trailhead.

some history

Turtle Mountain is a rich oasis of forest and small lakes that rises 245 metres from the surrounding grain fields. Nearly every open body of water in the park has at least one beaver lodge, and their dams are found wherever there is a semblance of natural drainage. In this manner the beaver in Turtle Mountain play a vital role in maintaining ponds and wildlife.

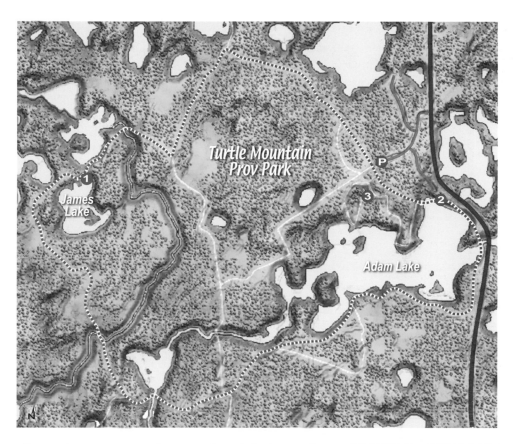

Beaver, however, were not always plentiful. In the early 1900s indiscriminate trapping had wiped out the beaver population here and by the 1930s many lakes had dried up due to the absence of these water engineers. Adam Lake was reduced to the size of a small pond.

In the 1940s beaver were successfully reintroduced and are now again so plentiful in the park that they are a nuisance. One simple device that prevents the beavers' harmful impact but still allows them to build and develop wetland ecosystems is the beaver deceiver. You will see these on many culverts along the trails. Essentially they consist of a caged filter that runs through the beaver dam and feeds a culvert. An upright drain is set at the maximum water surface elevation determined for the pond. When the pond reaches the maximum height set, water begins to flow through the culvert rather than continue to raise the pond water level and cause flooding. Since the beavers are unable to plug the caged filter, the desired water level is maintained.

P	*Park at the Adam Lake campground*
1	*James Lake cabin*
2	*causeway*
3	*Fitness trails*

some history

Lake Audy is home to a herd of bison who wander the Riding Mountain pastures much as they did in an earlier era. Before the arrival of European settlers, as many as 60 million bison roamed the vast North American plains. Bison are the largest land animal on this continent and were perfectly adapted to the rough grasses that grew on the prairies. A large herd would move across the plains clipping the grass down to sod. Sadly, by the 1890s, they were hunted to near extinction and at one point numbered less than a thousand.

In 1906, as part of a plan to rescue the animals, Ottawa purchased 700 plains bison from a private herd in Montana and established herds in several national parks. The captive herd at Lake Audy are descended from that original herd.

The first leg of the trail follows the bison enclosure, then west on the Central Trail before heading south through a stand of enormous white spruce. The forest then opens onto beautiful Grasshopper Valley which comes alive with thousands of flowers every spring and summer

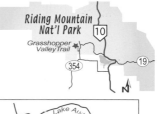

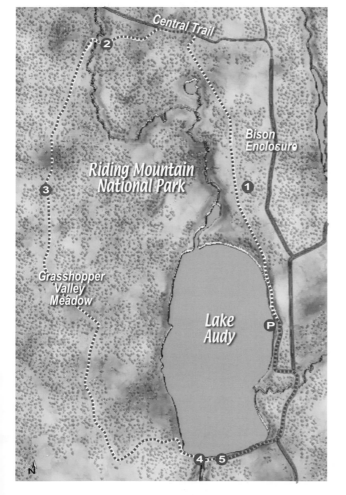

distance

20.5 km loop

P	Park at north end of Lake Audy camp ground
1	Bison enclosure
2	Minnedosa Creek campsite
3	Enter Grasshopper Valley meadow
4	Lake Audy dam
5	Follow roadway east & north back to parking

P	*Victoria Beach community parking lot*
1	*pump house*
2	*sand bar*
3	*trail to north shore*
4	*blueberry patch*

what you'll find

The island is six miles long and two and a half miles wide and was designated a provincial heritage park in 1974. The shoreline varies from sand beaches and limestone outcroppings on the south to a glacial boulder cliff shoreline on the north. The terrain rises in a series of benches from low-lying swamp on the southeast to a height of 112 feet on the northeast corner. The island is thickly forested with white spruce, jack pine, balsam and fir, and in the southeast corner, you'll find some of the best blueberry picking in the province.

how to get there

The only sanctioned parking is at the Victoria Beach community parking lot at the end of Hwy 59. From here you hike north on 8th St for 1.5 km then head northeast along a foot path that hugs the shoreline. This path heads inland. Follow McCord Drive north until you find another trail that goes back down to the water and leads to the point. From here, beckoning you, just a quarter mile offshore, is the majestic solitude of Elk Island.

Getting there is not always easy. If the water is warm and the wind calm, it's a fairly routine exercise to wade across. The trick is to negotiate the sand bar that connects the island with the mainland. For the most part, you'll have just two or three feet of water to deal with but when the waves are high, it can be difficult to find your footing. In fact, when conditions are unfavourable, it's foolhardy to even try. As always, great caution is advised.

Elk
Island

Victoria
Beach

59

11

distance

14 km loop

ELK ISLAND
PROVINCIAL
PARK

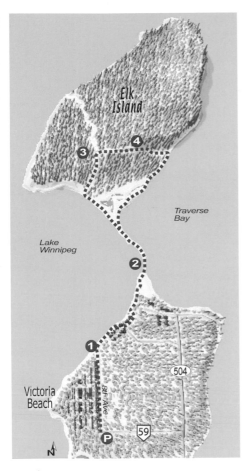

This island is near pristine wilderness with miles and miles of beautiful sandy beach. The park says that access is by boat only but many hardy souls wade across to the island every summer.

some history

From time immemorial, Elk Island has been a camping place for aboriginal people. The LaVerendrye explorers used it as a stopping off place as they travelled down the Winnipeg River, and the Wolseley Expedition, on their way from the East to crush the Riel rebellion, reportedly spent time here in 1870. Later residents included a few hardy loggers and fishermen, and from 1952 to 1969, a Faith Bible Camp. Today, development is limited to hiking and interpretive trails, and the island is returning to its original wilderness state.

Riding Mountain
Nat'l Park [10] [5]

Gorge
Creek
Trail

[19]

N

what's special

This narrow rugged trail plunges 1000 feet down the Manitoba Escarpment hugging the steep shale banks of the gorge. As you descend, the lush forest opens up providing remarkable vistas of the patchwork quilt farmland below.

distance

6.4 km one way / 12.8 km out & back

Note: The loose shale surface can be very slippery when wet.

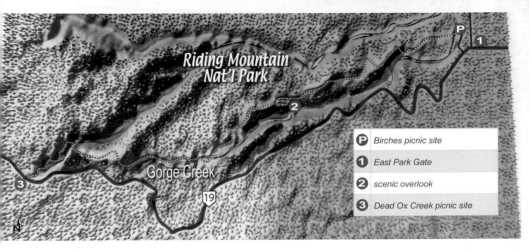

Riding Mountain
Nat'l Park

Gorge Creek

P Birches picnic site

1 East Park Gate

2 scenic overlook

3 Dead Ox Creek picnic site

what you'll find

This is a strenuous hike that is definitely worth the effort. We recommend you walk it both ways starting at the bottom – the Birches picnic site. The climb can be a definite struggle, particularly on a hot day, but the trail is so spectacular, it needs to be seen twice. If you do hike the trail one way only, we recommend starting at the top. Find parking at the Dead Ox Creek picnic site.

The vegetation along the trail goes through a series of changes. As you descend the escarpment, aspen forest gives way to bur oak, then Manitoba maple, elm and white birch. Note how the arid south and west-facing inclines support the oak and shrubs like hazelnut, chokecherry and saskatoon while the cool east and north-facing slopes tend to be aspen covered with birch and poplar occurring on moist sites.

what's special

This trail is a real work-out over some particularly rugged terrain, but the views are spectacular. You clamber up and down steep rock ridges that tower over the shorelines of Hunt Lake and West Hawk Lake. Brilliant green mosses border the pathway and wild iris wave at the water's edge.

This up-and-down trail parallels the shore, passing through beautiful pine & cedar forest then dropping down to a picnic shelter ❶ at the water's edge on Little Indian Bay - your destination for the hike.

some history

After crossing a cedar bog and you'll climb through a stand of white pine to higher ground. Here you'll catch your first sight of West Hawk Lake. Aside from being Manitoba's deepest lake, at 110 metres,

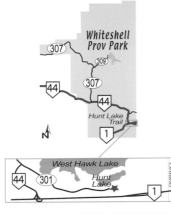

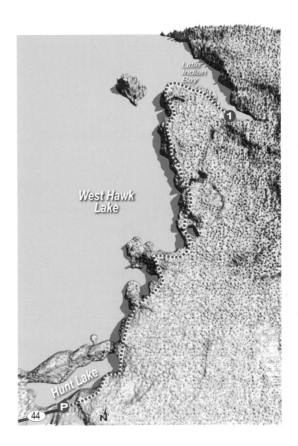

West Hawk can lay claim to an unusual birthright. In the distant past it was created when a meteor weighing more than a million tons collided with the earth. The evidence for this theory is that the lake is nearly circular, unusually deep, and the rock at its bottom has less density than the rock surrounding the lake. This crater lake is the last to lose its ice each spring. In the final stages of breakup, the small porous

distance

6.5 km one way / 13 km out & back

chunks of ice collide continuously, making a giant wind chime out of the lake's surface.

The up-and-down trail continues to parallel the shore, passing through more beautiful pine forest. Then the trail drops down to a picnic shelter ❶ at the water's edge on Little Indian Bay and you have reached your destination.

Epinette Creek - Newfoundland Trail

This trail showcases the scenic diversity of Spruce Woods. It's a blend of spruce parkland, mixed-grass prairie, sand dune and riverbottom forest. You're taken up and down steep valley walls and rewarded with breathtaking views of the Assiniboine River Valley below.

what you'll find

This is a well marked and maintained semi-wilderness loop trail of moderate difficulty.

distance

Our map shows a 19.4 km portion of the 40 km loop.

campsites

5 primitive campsites along the trail

how to get there

Find the Epinette trailhead off Hwy 5 in the north end of the park.

Spruce Woods
Prov Park

5

Assiniboine River

N

some history

Something very remarkable began here over a century ago when one 'larger than life' character by the name of Ernest Thompson Seton came on the scene. Seton who was a struggling artist, travelled here to join his brothers who were homesteading near Carberry. He tried his hand at farming but was constantly distracted by his natural surroundings. For weeks on end he would roam these hills, recording images of the wildlife around him. He also wrote stories about animals and gave birth to a new literary genre. His books 'The Trail of the Sand Hill Stag' and 'Wild Animals I Have Known' became wildly popular, were read all over the world and in many ways, changed the way people viewed nature. Stories were told from the animal's point of view with animals invested

with such human qualities as curiosity, desire and sympathy.

In his lifetime Seton achieved great renown as a wildlife illustrator and a naturalist who was also a spell-binding storyteller and lecturer. Although his books

brought him worldwide fame and fortune (they are read to this day), he always credited the Carberry Sand Hills as the source of his finest inspiration and his days spent here the happiest of his life.

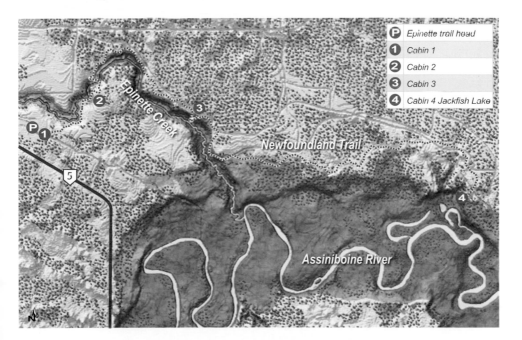

P Epinette trail head
1 Cabin 1
2 Cabin 2
3 Cabin 3
4 Cabin 4 Jackfish Lake

Epinette Creek

Newfoundland Trail

Assiniboine River

Kwasitchewan Falls

This trail begins at picturesque Pisew Falls and follows the thickly forested shoreline of the Grass River out to a series of rapids and then on to Kwasitchewan, Manitoba's highest falls. For most of the trail the waters of the Grass River are within sight.

what you'll find

This is a rugged backcountry trail, recommended only for an experienced hiker. Rock surfaces are slippery when wet and there are a few wet, boggy stretches, especially in spring and after heavy rains. A 0.5 km trail leads to the Rotary Bridge over the Grass River below Pisew Falls. The bridge gives access to trails to the top of Pisew Falls & to the 22 km trail leading to Kwasitchewan Falls.

distance

22 km loop

campsites

Primitive campsite near Kwasitchewan Falls

how to get there

The short turn off to Pisew Falls is 66 km south of Thompson on Hwy 6.

some history

This trail follows the Grass River, the key waterway in the late 1700s fur trade route known as the Upper Track. Aboriginal people, who had travelled this route for thousands of years, showed traders from Hudson Bay, that they could reach the Saskatchewan River and the interior of western Canada by this route. Along the Grass, competition between the "Bay' men and North West Company traders was intense during 1790's and early 1800's as both companies vied for the bulk of the furs.

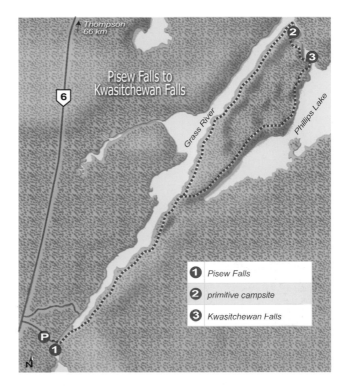

Pisew Falls to Kwasitchewan Falls

Thompson
66 km

Grass River

Phillips Lake

1 Pisew Falls

2 primitive campsite

3 Kwasitchewan Falls

RIDING MOUNTAIN

some history

Riding Mountain National Park is an island of protected wilderness that rises dramatically from the prairie floor below. Early fur traders termed this a mountain as they viewed its summit rising 1500 feet from the flat lands below. They probably added the word 'riding' because it was in this general vicinity that they changed from canoes to saddle horses to continue their travels westward.

This rolling plateau that forms part of the Manitoba Escarpment, stands at the crossroads of three habitats. High areas are covered with forests of spruce, jack-pine, balsam fir and tamarack intermingled with stands of aspen and groves of white birch; along the base of the escarpment, the richer soils support forests of hardwoods as well as shrubs, vines and ferns. In the western part of the reserve, you'll find large areas of grasslands and meadow, where a galaxy of wildflowers can be found.

These blends of vegetation and topography support an almost equally varied number of animals. The home of bison before their near extinction, the park was allocated a small herd of these great beasts soon after its creation. Today you can view bison roaming the park on a partly forested grassland plain near Lake Audy.

what you'll find

The best way to experience this magnificent park is to spend a night or two camping out under the stars. The park's habitat varies from the rugged gorges of the east side of the park to the tall evergreens and meadows of the western portion. The park guide lists more trails and campsites than what we've shown here. We're highlighting two distinctly different groups of trails. They are the most popular backcountry trails in the park and they are interconnecting, allowing you to design a route to suit yourself.

Trail surfaces vary from partially gravelled patrol roads to grassy trails. Wet conditions may be encountered, particularly in the spring. Flooding on the trails, caused by beaver dams, is occasionally a problem.

You must obtain a permit for camping in the backcountry of Riding Mountain. For permits call 204.848-7275. Up-to-date information on trails or backcountry camping is available at the Visitor Centre.

North Escarpment

The North Escarpment Trail serves as a connector to Bald Hill, Packhorse, & J.E.T. Trails which can all be part of a scenic backpacking tour. It parallels the edge of the Manitoba Escarpment and passes over the highest point in the park. Charred trees along the way show evidence of a past fire. The Bald Hill & Packhorse Trails are primarily on an old roads that follows the Bald Hill Creek Valley off the Manitoba Escarpment. They have several steep sections and excellent views of the deeply cut gorge and the farmland below.

The J.E.T. Trail follows the ridge separating the gorges carrying Bald Hill and Packhorse Creeks and passes 3 reservoirs and Lake Ritchie. Once past the ridge reservoir the trail begins a steep descent until reaching a gravel pit. Two spur trails lead to viewpoints. There are steep ascents and descents.

what you'll find

distance

North Escarpment Trail 8.4 km (one way)
Bald Hill Trail 8.8 km (one way)
Packhorse Trail 11 km (one way)
J.E.T. Trail 7.3 km (one way)

campsites

2 primitive campsites along the trail

how to get there

Southern trailhead on Hwy 19 approx 2 km west of Dead Ox Creek picnic site.

Central Trail

This former patrol road provides the main access into the western half of the park and takes you deep into backcountry. The trail passes through a variety of landscapes from dense stands of white spruce or aspen, to open rolling grasslands. It connects up with the park's premier scenic wilderness hikes (Tilson Lake, Birdtail Valley & Sugarloaf Hills) allowing a variety of options for your route.

The Tilson Lake loop is a physically demanding trail offering a splendid mix of vegetation and a good contrast in topography. Expect steep hills and lovely fescue meadows.

The Sugarloaf Trail gets you into the Sugarloaf Hills a.k.a. the Birdtail Bench, with views of the high rolling hills found along either side of the beautiful Birdtail Valley. (See pg 170)

Some of the best scenery of the park is found along the Birdtail Trail. It has tremendous variety with a combination of mixed forest and meadow. From Kay's campsite you climb over the southern hills of the Birdtail valley where the landscape opens into prairie and the trail joins part of the historic Angusville Trail.

what you'll find

distance

Central Trail - 67 km (one way)
Tilson Lake Trail - 38.5 km loop
Sugarloaf Trail - 8 km (one way)
Birdtail Trail - 11.4 km (one way)

campsites

primitive campsites at - Whitewater Lake / Gunn Creek / Deep Lake / Long Lake / Gunn Lake / Birdtail / Tilson Lake / Kays

how to get there

The eastern trailhead is at the north end of the Bison enclosure at Lake Audy. The western trailhead is at the Deep Lake Warden Station.

Whiteshell Provincial Park

Whiteshell Provincial Park lies at the southern edge of Manitoba's Precambrian Shield, a wild and beautiful land of granite ridges, lush pine forests, and crystal clear lakes. When Manitobans say cottage country, more often than not they think of the Whiteshell. This is our most popular spot for summer cabins. With its 2800 square kilometres of protected wilderness, this is our largest and most visited park.

Trail into George Lake (See Map Page 86)

This hike winds through a particularly scenic part of the park, crossing an ocean of rock surrounded by lush forest. You'll find your destination at a wilderness campsite where Tie Creek tumbles into the pristine clarity of George Lake.

what you'll find

Our route begins on an old cart track now used by ATVs or 'quads'. This is not an official park trail, there are no trail markers. The beginning and end sections of the hike take us through lush forest of spruce and birch. Expect some muddy areas and makeshift bridges.

distance

11.5 km one way / 23 km out & back

campsites

primitive campsite on the shore of George Lake

how to get there

Find this trail off PR 307 between Bannock Point petroforms and Pine Point Rapids trail. The turnoff has a stop sign and is marked ER31.

Christel Bischoff

Mantario Trail

Developed by the Manitoba Naturalists Society in 1970s, the Mantario showcases a wilderness characterized by rugged granite ridges, deep clear lakes and lush forests. It is the longest such trail in the Canadian Shield in Western Canada and attracts hikers from all over the world.

what you'll find

It is intended for the experienced backpacker in good shape and is considered a gruelling four day work-out and too arduous for children. In places the trail may be overgrown and difficult to follow. Other challenges may include wet, slippery rocks, beaver dams and scrambles up high rock ridges.

distance

66 km
Typical backpacker takes about 30 hours over 3 or 4 days to complete the trail.

campsites

Campsites located at Caribou Lake, Marion Lake, Olive Lake, Moosehead Lake, Mantario Lake, Ritchey Lake, Hemenway Lake & Big Whiteshell Lake. These are all primitive campsites with no amenities except for steel fire pits.

Whiteshell Prov Park

how to get there

The south trailhead is off Hwy 312 east of Caddy Lake and the north trailhead on the north shore of Big Whiteshell Lake at the end of Hwy 309.

A trail map is essential for this hike and is available for purchase through Manitoba Naturalists 204.943-9029 or Canada Map Sales toll free 877.627-7226

Roaring River Canyon

A true outback adventure! You'll trek through dense forest dotted with beautiful upland meadows, vivid with lush green grasses and strewn with wild flowers throughout spring and summer.

what you'll find

This hike gets you into some very scenic and unspoiled backcountry in the northern part of Duck Mountain Provincial Forest. The route travels a combination of forestry roads and age-old foot paths. There are no trail markers. The first section of trail is a newly cut road allowance that runs west towards the river. Next you'll take up an ancient Indian path that follows the Roaring River. This trail winds through thick forest broken by lovely open prairie and offers some lovely views of the valley.

You'll ford the river (which can be dicey when the water is high) and pass through beautiful Jumper Plains, then on to a trapper's cabin on Teepee Creek. A return route along the east side of the creek gets you back following Roaring River trail through the Heart Hill part of the canyon and beyond. This south part of the route along the river with a view of the steep sloping valley walls, is the most scenic portion of the hike. We've made a circle route so that you can return a different way but the north half of the route gets you into some clear-cut areas and much of it is badly chewed up by ATVs.

This area is popular with hunters and fishermen. Most come in by ATV but we've seen a few people on horseback.

Be aware that treaty rights allow year round hunting by First Nations. Conservation Manitoba suggests wearing something orange year round.

distance

32 km loop

campsites

One fairly established campsite on the north bank of the Roaring River just to the west of the ford. Most people like to pick their own spot at the edge of a meadow or near a stream. No open fires!

how to get there

You'll find a newly cut road allowance running west about 2 km to meet up with an old pathway that skirts the Roaring River.

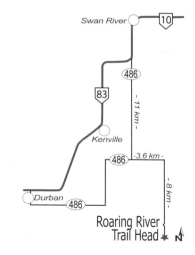

Swan River — 10

486

83 — 11 km —

Kenville

486 — 3.6 km —

Durban 486 — 8 km —

Roaring River
Trail Head N

some history

The Duck Mountain Forest is a unique area of natural meadows, streams and wetlands amid a forest complex containing both softwoods and hardwoods, including black and white spruce, jackpine and tamarac, birch, trembling aspen and poplar.

Much of the forest you'll see along this trail is in various states of regrowth. Parts have been logged out and parts have been destroyed by fire. In fact 85% of the Duck Mountain forest was burned in the drought years of 1885 to 1895.

Logging has always been an important industry in the area. Recently Louisiana Pacific, a major multi-national firm, has moved into the Ducks bringing with it some sophisticated harvesting practices with emphasis on sustainable forestry. They consider the practice of clear-cutting the most viable method of harvesting logs and they also think that it best mimics the effects of a forest fire. In strategic areas, "skips" or patches of forest that a fire bypasses, are left untouched. As well, buffer zones along waterways and sensitive areas like Jumper Plains are left alone. The open space of the clear cut gives jackpine and black spruce enough light and warmth to regrow and in theory keeps the forest healthy.

This is not a subject without controversy and in the short term, hiking through a forest that is open to logging means that scenic values suffer

in the interests of the economy. A new clearcut is not a pleasant sight but in 3 to 4 years the area is green again and pleasant enough to walk through and in 10-14 years the replanted trees are as much as 35 feet tall. Every 70 to 100 years the trees can be harvested and the cycle begins again

	WAYPOINTS
51°53'44.2"N, 101°13'25.9"W	**P** Park & take new trail leading west
51°53'38.7"N, 101°15'17.9"W	**1** turn south
51°50'34.9"N, 101°11'48.3"W	**2** trapper's cabin
51°51'47.7"N, 101°10'44.9"W	**3** spring
51°51'48.5"N, 101°7'10.2"W	**4** intersection with Wellman Lake Rd
51°52'58.8"N, 101°10'06.0"W	**5** intersection with Fuller Trail

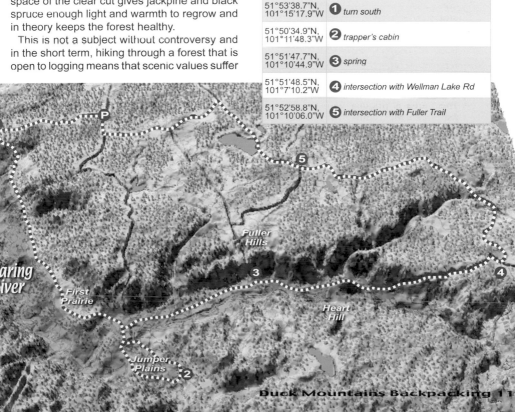

Jumper-Plains in July

distance

3 km loop

some history

Before 1915, ancient foot paths provided the only access to these slopes but when this was designated Forest Preserve, the building of fire roads became top priority.

what's special

A lookout tower at the trailhead offers up a dramatic 360-degree view of forests and distant farms from the highest point in the province.

Forest Rangers patrolled the road on horseback, on foot or by team and wagon and worked continuously to keep the trails passable for summer travel. Cabins and barns were built throughout the Ducks for use by these Rangers and many of those buildings remain standing. You'll encounter two of these old cabins and a barn along the trail.

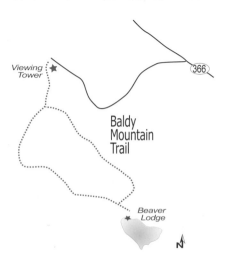

distance

1.4 km loop

Pick up a brochure/map for this self-guiding trail at the trailhead.

what's special

You'll climb the southern wall of the valley carved by the old Assiniboine River, ascending through marshy wetland up onto an arid ridge. A panoramic view of distant sand dunes and forest awaits you at the top.

Spruce Woods Prov Park

5 Assiniboine River

Isputinaw Trail

N

PRAIRIE SHORE NATURE TRAIL

distance

1.6 km loop

Pick up a brochure/map for this self-guiding trail at the trail head.

what's special

This trail forms a loop through native prairie, sedge meadow and aspen and oak woodland.

You are entering an endangered ecosystem, a plant and animal community so rare that less than 1% of it still exists in the world. This is part of one of the last remnants of the tall-grass prairie. At one time tall-grass prairie was a vast sea of waving grasses & wildflowers extending from southern Manitoba to Texas.

distance

3.2 km loop

Pick up a brochure/map for this self-guiding trail at the trail head.

to Flin Flon

Grass River Prov Park

★ Karst Springs

Cranberry Portage

39

N 10

what's special

This lovely and peaceful trail follows the Grass River upstream climbing a ridge that forms a divide between the Manitoba Lowlands and the Precambrian Shield. At the halfway point of the trail, interpretive signs lead you to a rich carpet of emerald green moss and lichens where an underwater spring erupts from a limestone rock face.

what's special

Attractively designed boardwalks and colourful interpretive signs designed to especially appeal to children, take a fun approach to educating about the forest and the creatures that inhabit it. You'll hike through the thick stands of spruce, fir, pine and tamarack that cover much of Riding Mountain and you'll gain a new understanding of our northern or boreal forest.

Riding Mountain
Nat'l Park

Boreal
Trail

10

19

N

distance

1 km loop

distance

.9 km one way / 1.8 km out & back

Pick up a brochure/map for this self-guiding trail at the trail head.

some ancient history

Nopiming Provincial Park, a semi-wilderness preserve, is 1250 sq km of rugged terrain underlined with granite and green with pine, spruce and aspen. Bedrock in the park dates back to the Precambrian Era more than 2 billion years ago. This is the oldest rock on earth. It's hard to believe, but this was once part of an immense mountain range, similar to the Rocky Mountains. Over time, the ancient peaks were worn down by wind, rain and the weight of ice. When the last ice age ended about 10,000 years ago, it left behind the raw new landscape you see today.

what you'll find

This is a moderately difficult hike leading to a magnificent 360° view which includes Tooth Lake. The trail surface is mainly bedrock with several short steep inclines. Some stairs have been provided.

FORESTER'S FOOTSTEPS

distance

2.4 km loop

Pick up a brochure/map for this self-guiding trail at the trail head.

what you'll find

This is a pleasant walk with a wide variety of trees and flowers on display. It loops through a natural forest as well as a Jack Pine plantation. Most of the trail follows old logging roads, except the last third which goes up a granite rock ridge. Part of the trail is designated as a mountain bike trail.

Whiteshell Prov Park

Forester's Footsteps Trail

distance

2.4 km loop

Pick up a campground map at the park office. This is the 'Bobolink Trail' Start at group picnic shelter & walk east along the lake to the spillway.

what's special

Nestled on the shores of Stephenfield Lake, adjacent to some of Manitoba's richest farmland, this quiet family park will surprise you with its beauty.

Our route loops out from the group picnic shelter along the lakeshore to explore the unique spillway and fish ladder that drains into the Boyne River at the east end of the park. This is a favourite spot for fishermen.

Stephenfield Prov Park
13
Carman
245
3
← 23 km →
3
N

Riding Mountain Nat'l Park

Bead Lakes Trail

distance

4 km loop

what you'll find

Bead Lakes is named for the chain of small lakes found at its mid-point. This trail offers an excellent opportunity to see a wide variety of wildlife. It climbs a large ridge and passes through a mature white birch forest, and an understory of hazel, young aspen and white spruce.

Between the lakes you'll see how beaver dams have dramatically affected lake levels.

distance

2 km loop

Pick up a brochure/map for this self-guiding trail at the trail head.

some history

Lakes, like living things, have a life-cycle. Through time, old lakes become new meadows. The abundant annual growth of vegetation is one major reason why this lake will become a meadow one day. As plants die and decompose they add organic material to the bottom of this depression. Another source of fill is inorganic material, like clay, washed down by rain from surrounding slopes. Each year the lake becomes shallower. When the water becomes sufficiently shallow, emergent plants like cattails and horsetails begin to grow.

what's special

Interpretive signs along this short trail, describe the life of a Turtle Mountain lake and how it eventually disappears. People often see moose, waterfowl, beaver and other wildlife.

NARCISSE SNAKE DENS

(EASY FAMILY WALKS)

when to go

The best viewing times are during the later part of April and first two weeks in May. The greatest activity tends to coincide with the disappearance of snow and the first few hot sunny days of spring.

Garter snakes return to their dens in early September. Once there, they remain active and visible to visitors until cool, wet autumn weather forces them underground. Fall viewing of snakes is best during warm sunny days.

some history

One explanation for the snake pits in this region is the Interlake's limestone bedrock, soft and easily eroded by ground water, which can become riddled with tunnels or even caves which collapse and become sinkholes. Some measure 75 feet across and 15 feet deep, allowing the snakes to hibernate below the frost line.

what's special

The Narcisse Snake Dens come alive with snakes for two brief periods each year. Here you can see more garter snakes at a glance than anywhere else in the world.

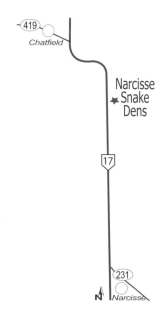

distance

3 km loop

Pick up a brochure/map for this self-guiding trail at the trail head.

Ancient Valley Trail

distance

3 km loop

Pick up a brochure/map for these self-guiding trails at the park office.

Asessippi
Prov Park

Ancient
Valley Trail

83

482

what's special

This self-guiding trail winds up wooded slopes to open prairie that is dotted with wild flowers from spring to fall. Interpretive signs along the way help you explore glacial features that were created over 8500 years ago and the results of erosion that continue to change today's Assiniboine River valley wall.

Shell River Loop Trail

distance

0.4 km one way /
0.8 km out & back

Walk past the play ground & picnic site down a sandy track past the sign marked 'Shell River Loop'. Take the steep trail down to the water. This offers some excellent views!

distance

1.5 km loop

some history

The attractive picnic grounds at the edge of this oxbow lake was once the farmstead of the Marsh family. The Marshs were one of the many families who homesteaded in the area in the 1870s. Unfortunately by 1895, it became clear that the land had very poor agricultural potential and the provincial government decided to conserve the area by designating it a Forest Reserve. In 1964 the eastern portion of this forest became a provincial park.

The signs along the trail allow hikers to explore this oxbow lake and the life around it.

Wekusko Falls

15 km

392

100 km
to The Pas

39

what's special

Wekusko Falls Provincial Park is one of the prettiest spots along the Grass River and a nature lover's dream. The river plunges almost 12 metres through a series of falls and rapids. This walk showcases the cascading water with two suspension foot bridges crossing the river making a loop. Another path leads you to the beautiful campgrounds spread out along the water.

This is a Prairie Pathfinder favourite - We give it four stars!

distance

3 km loop / Pick up a campground map at the park office.

distance

5 km loop

some history

This trail is on land that was once a rocky beach ridge of the glacial Lake Agassiz, formed more than 12,000 years ago. The land was too rocky to be valuable farmland, so most of it was left for livestock grazing. That allowed for the preservation of the precious remnants of the tall-grass prairie located in the southeastern part of the province.

what's special

The trail is home to 6 foot tall big bluestem, wetlands, exotic sandhill cranes, aspen forest, 2 different endangered orchids and the brilliant red-orange prairie lily.

what you'll find

This is a narrow foot path though dense forest. Much of it has that wonderful spongy moss surface. It skirts the lake then climbs a high thickly wooded ridge giving you a series of scenic overlooks.

Listen for the call of the loon!

Duck Mountain Prov Park

Spray Lake Trail

366

367

366

N

366

Spray Lake

Spray Lake Trail

N

distance

3.5 km loop

what's special

High rocky cliffs and a pristine shoreline make this a beautiful place to explore. Clearwater Lake is well named - you can see the bottom at 36 feet. Perfect white rounded stones gleam in the aquamarine waters.

With a series of stairways and viewing platforms, the trail weaves down and around deep cave-like crevices in the dolomite bedrock. These caves were formed when rock masses split away from shoreline cliffs. In the dark, cool depths it's not unusual to find ice as late as July.

Scramble down a path in a crevice to the shoreline where you can look up at the caves from the waters edge.

Clearwater Lake
Prov Park

Caves Trail

10
287
384

The Pas

N

distance

0.8 km loop

Pick up a brochure/map for this self-guiding trail at the trail head.

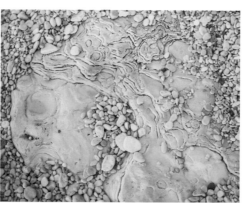

distance

4.8 km loop

what you'll find

This trail takes you over densely forested rock ridges and across boardwalks through swamp. It leads to a large high expanse of rock outcrop that overlooks the Rennie River. From here a side trail leads to the beach at Inverness Falls.

FYI

Part of this trail overlaps the Trans Canada Trail and you may find the signage confusing. A number of people have reported difficulty in finding the return path from the rocky outcrop. Just remember that you need to go southeast. This return part of the loop is particularly scenic.

FIRE OF 83

Fire
of '83
Trail

314

ONTARIO

Nopiming
Prov Park

315

distance

1.5 km loop

Pick up a brochure/map for this self-guiding trail at the trail head.

some history

Nopiming Provincial Park is a tiny fragment of a forest that stretches from Alaska to Newfoundland. Much of it between northern Saskatchewan & Canada's east coast is on an ancient rock foundation and is known as the Precambrian boreal forest. You are about to explore a rocky upland (also rock outcrop) which is typical of the landscape.

As you walk upon these outcrops, you'll notice veins of white quartz that attracted gold prospectors in the 1920s.

The Precambrian boreal forest is well adapted to and dependent on periodic visits from fire to maintain its vitality and wildlife diversity. Fire naturally started by lightning has been a force of change and renewal since the forest appeared here about 8000 years ago.

Plants and animals in this forest are familiar with fire - it has been part of the boreal forest picture for thousands of years. A fire swept through this area in September 1983. After a prolonged drought, lightning sparked a blaze that raged for weeks, eventually burning out 98 square miles. Today, the brilliant shimmering green of new growth forest makes a colourful contrast against the rock.

what's special

This hike up one of the park's highest hills brings you to a picnic site and viewing tower offering a spectacular northward view of Glad Lake.

At the summit you'll find a monument to Nicolaus Copernicus, the Polish astronomer who in the early 1500s discovered that the earth (and other planets) go around the sun rather than vice versa. A plaque describes his work that changed the course of human history.

Duck Mountain Prov Park

Copernicus Hill

366

367

366

N

distance

1.5 km loop

distance

6 km one way / 12 km out & back
some steep climbs

Silver
Bend
Trail

old railway
bridge

Assiniboine River

2 km

83

Miniota

N 24

how to get there

Turn off Hwy#83, (just behind the Miniota town sign) and drive west as far as road conditions permit. Cross the high wooden railway bridge on foot and continue along the cart track to the Silver Bend trailhead sign.

some history

The community of Miniota built this trail to celebrate the early settlement history of the Assiniboine River. As you trek along the edge of the valley, a colourful past is brought to life. The trail passes Doyle's Landing where steamboats unloaded supplies from Winnipeg in the late 1880s. It passes the gravestone of Charles Hillyar, son of Admiral Hillyar, who drowned when he fell off the back of the steamboat in 1883. You'll see a wooden cross nailed to a sturdy oak tree which marks the graves of Dr. Rolston's two children who contracted smallpox from passengers on the boat and died.

what's special

This hike takes you up and down steep valley walls, through thick oak forest and out onto wildflower meadows with spectacular valley overlooks. Interpretive signage along the way brings stories from the past to life.

The trail ends at a tarpaper shack and a lookout over the valley. This old shack with its weatherbeaten siding was the home of Mrs Samuel Babiuk. She raised a family of ten here in the early part of the last century and she lived here well into her late 70s.

🅿	Park Lake parking lot
❶	trail intersection / Turn right
❷	Doyle's Landing
❸	Babiuk cabin

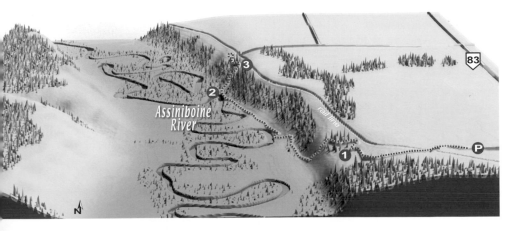

CAMP MORTON

8 km loop

what's special

Our route meanders in and out of thick forest atop a rocky ledge overlooking Lake Winnipeg. You'll pass some highly unusaul historic buildings and formal gardens of Camp Morton.

some history

Years ago these woods were full of the sound of children playing all summer long.

Camp Morton Prov Park

324

222

Lake Winnipeg

P Camp Morton parking lot

1 Stackwall cottages

2 camping / picnic site

Steeple Trail

Birch Trail

Moon shine Trail

N

Two 'fresh air' camps for underprivileged kids, were established here after World War I. A Monsignor Morton set up a Catholic camp that bore his name in 1920 and further south along the shore, the Union Bank founded the

nondenominational Lakeside Camp as a philanthropic effort in tribute to the fallen soldiers of WWI. These summer holidays were a godsend for the kids. Most had never been swimming or even outside the city before. Besides the obvious benefits to their health and happiness, the camps served as a process of acculturation into Canadian society for these immigrant children from the urban ghettos.

Originally Camp Morton included 14 cottages built of "stackwall" - a method of construction using short sections of logs laid horizontally like bricks and secured with mortar fill. The logs were soaked overnight in a solution of bluestone to reduce shrinkage in the wood. Then they were laid in rows between vertical posts fastened to a concrete foundation. The wall with its "block and lime" mortar was allowed to harden and then was capped with a plank top plate to which the roof rafters were attached. The method of construction was cheap and since the area had a surplus of small poplar logs, it became a popular design.

By the 1960s, changes in society and a decline in interest led to the closure of the camps but in 1974, Camp Morton and adjacent lands were designated a provincial recreational park. The grounds and buildings are now maintained by the department of Natural Resources and the formal park in Camp Morton is a must-see for any garden enthusiast. Volunteers from the Gimli Women's Institute assist in maintaining a lovely sunken garden with a sundial and walkways lined with flower urns.

```
        (340)
           - ≈ 3 km -
                        ★
              Criddle
              / Vane
   Assiniboine   Homestead
            River

(453)   N      Treesbank
               Ferry
```

distance

2.2 km total

0.8 km loop + 1.4 km loop

A pamphlet published by the Criddle / Vane Homestead Heritage Committee is available at the site. It contains maps and details points of interest.

some history

This hike loops around the Criddle/Vane homestead where a pale box-shaped house still stands. The story of this remarkable pioneer family would be judged too far-fetched if written as fiction and has all the elements of a first rate melodrama.

In 1882, Percy Criddle was a merchant in London. He was a master of several languages and educated in law, medicine and music. His wife Alice was one of the first female scholars of Cambridge University.

The Criddles enjoyed a refined and cultured life. They were accomplished musicians, composers, naturalists, and astronomers. But at age 38, Percy decided quite suddenly to leave the comforts of England behind, emigrate to Manitoba and begin farming. His family fortune was depleted and Canada, no doubt, represented his best escape from

Christel Bischoff

These two trails which loop through woods and meadow, are dotted with interpretive signage that celebrates one of Manitoba's most unusual and remarkable pioneer families and their outstanding contributions to the field of science and culture.

a failing business. Perhaps judging the challenges ahead insufficient, Percy booked passage not only for his wife and their four offspring, but also (in steerage class) his second family of five children and mistress Elise Vane. According to legend, wife Alice was to learn of this extra-marital arrangement only as their ship set sail.

Whatever painful misgivings both Alice and Elise must have suffered, both women clearly decided to make the best of a bad lot. The Criddle resources were limited, and Percy had no skill as a farmer. It was left to the women and children to care for the animals and tend the fields. Percy concerned himself with living the life of a gentleman and bringing civilization to the prairies. He handed over the management of all field work to eldest son Edwys, aged 11.

Those first few years were bitterly hard. Food was scarce, and the climate was a shock to them. Percy spent his time playing the violin and building a tennis court. Without the resourcefulness and cooperation of his two wives, both families would have undoubtedly starved. Against all odds, the Criddles and Vanes flourished.

Combining their talents and abilities, they created a home where the children thrived and often excelled. Their home was to become a valuable place of science, and the Criddle name recognized for accomplishments in botany, biology and natural history. Son Norman Criddle was appointed Dominion Entomologist for Manitoba, and brother Stuart was awarded an honorary Doctor of Science degree for his work in biology. Norman credited his mother for his accomplishments and ability as a scientist. While Elise took over the practical matters of running a household, Alice was able to give an unusual breadth of education to all the children.

In time, Percy's dream of a cultured country estate began to take shape. To accompany their tennis court, they laid out a cricket pitch and nine-hole golf course. They acquired a fine library, a billiard table, an organ and a prized telescope. Their home was dubbed St Albans and became a centre for social activity in the district as neighbours gathered for sports tournaments, dances and a choral society organized by Percy.

Just south of the abandoned homestead, you'll find a private cemetery nestled under large spruce trees and surrounded by a wire fence. At the back are two identical heart shaped headstones - Percy Criddle (1844-1918) and Alice Criddle

(1849-1918). Nearby the stone for Elise Vane (1839-1903) offers the only suggestion of the remarkable nature of this family's story.

Norman's laboratory is the only other building on this homestead that remains standing. Norman Criddle, probably the most well known member of the family, developed a keen and abiding interest in his natural surroundings at a very young age. In 1902, during a serious grasshopper outbreak, Norman became quite famous for producing the 'Criddle Mixture', a poison compound that was accepted by

children learned to coax birds to perch on their heads and shoulders, and to feed unafraid from their hands. They became true advocates of preserving wildlife to enjoy and show others. An early visitor to St Albans was sternly admonished to 'enjoy the wildflowers, admire them all as much as you like, but whatever you do, don't pick so much as one of them". We recommend this same practice to visitors to the homestead today as they trace the footprints of this fascinating pioneer family.

the Dominion Department of Agriculture as a proven weapon against the rapacious insects. Later Norman added an 'east wing' to his laboratory to provide overnight accommodation for the many visiting scientists who came to consult with him.

Percy Criddle's diaries record the discoveries of all the prairie plants and animals that were new to them. Special notes were made of the wild roses that bloomed in such profusion throughout the summer, the crocus-like anemones and the 'red lilies'. The Criddle

FYI

As with all great stories, new elements continue to be unearthed. A fresh interpretation of events will soon be published by Elise Vane's great granddaughter, Oriole Vane Veldhuis. Oriole has been doing extensive research in Britain and Germany for the past six years and her account promises to challenge many of our assumptions about the characters in this drama.

what's special

This section of Trans Canada Trail runs from the magnificent ruins of the Old Pinawa Dam site to the spectacular Pinawa Suspension bridge upstream. The first section, mainly a new trail, winds though woods and wildflower meadow while much of the last part is on an old cart track. Served up all along the track are intermittent views of the jutting rock and sparkling water of Pinawa Channel.

Old Pinawa Dam Heritage Park

Pinawa Channel

520

211   Pinawa   N

distance

8.6 km one way / 17.2 km out & back

some history

The rushing waters of the Pinawa Channel race up to the ruins of an early engineering wonder. This is the site of Manitoba's first year round hydro-electric dam. For fifty years starting in 1906, it served up the power supply for the growing city of Winnipeg. The town of Old Pinawa was beautifully laid out on the side of the hill. This was a busy and self-contained community with pretty brick houses and fine public buildings.

In 1951 the power plant was shut down so that the full flow of the Winnipeg River could be restored to the main channel for use by the newly expanded Seven Sisters Dam.

Today the site is a jumbled mass of masonry resembling the ruins of a ancient Roman viaduct.

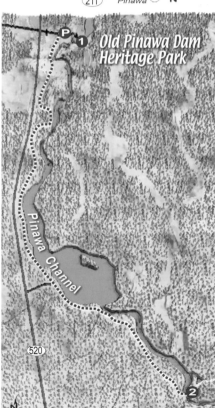

P 1

Old Pinawa Dam Heritage Park

Pinawa Channel

520

2

distance

4 km one way / 8 km out & back

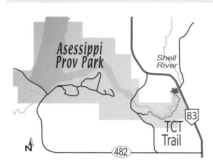

Asessippi Prov Park

Shell River

83

TCT Trail

482

N

some history

All ghost towns carry an aura of mystery but Asessippi is particularly perplexing. In the early 1880s it was a boom town promising to be the new industrial centre of the west. It was a bustling frontier community with saw mill, brick factory, cheese plant and grist and flour mill. The famous Fort Pelly Trail was rerouted to pass through its streets. The Shell River provided a ready source of water and power, the land was well-suited for agriculture, and an abundant supply of timber was at hand. No town had a brighter beginning nor a more picturesque setting.

In 1886, it was dealt a blow when the Manitoba and North Western Railway reneged on its promise to continue through the Shell Valley and stopped 12 miles south at Russell. As with so many towns of this era,

what's special

You'll hike through what is probably the most beautiful ghost town site in Manitoba with spectacular views of the Shell River Valley all around.

expansion and prosperity depended on this rail link. To Asessippi, this was a considerable setback, but the sudden collapse of the town is still hard to understand. By 1890, Asessippi was dying and only a handful of settlers hung on until 1914. Today the rusty remains of a bridge and several dilapidated buildings are all that survive of this once thriving town.

Climbing the steep valley wall you'll eventually reach the Asessippi Ski Hill. This is a snazzy new multi-million dollar resort that has terrific facilities for snow-boarders and skiers alike. You're welcome to explore the area off-season. Some of the runs make excellent hikes and give you a terrific view of the valley.

Find the turn-off that runs west off Hwy 83 just south of the Shell River. Drive in and park to the side of the road. The trail is marked with Trans Canada Trail signs.

P	*Drive in and park to the side of the road*
1	*Asessippi townsite*
2	*Asessippi Ski Resort*

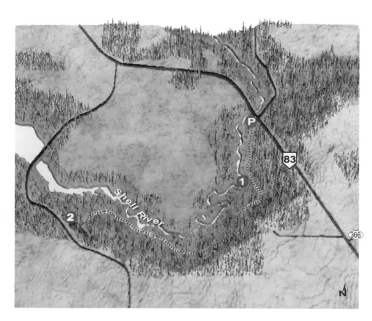

Venlaw

Negrych
Homestead

274

10

- 3.2 km -

- 4.3 km -

17.3 km
to Gilbert
Plains

Drifting River

N

to
Dauphin

one mile
one km

some history

Your approach to the homestead, a winding lane bordered by poplar and spruce, leads you into a remarkable set of Ukrainian folk buildings and a glimpse into a vanished way of life.

Four Negrych families emigrated here from the western highlands of Ukraine in the late 1890s. They established their farmsteads in the middle of the section thus creating a sort of miniature village. Today, the isolation of the place adds to its aura of authenticity.

The main site of original log farm buildings which stand much as they always have, was home to Wasyl and Anna Negrych and their 13 children. The log buildings, some dating back to 1897, were constructed with materials found at hand, using ancient folk

what's special

This hike loops around one of the most scenic and best preserved heritage sites in North America!

building techniques. Spruce and tamarack logs were joined at the corners with saddle notch joints. Then walls were coated with mud and clay.

One feature unique in Ukrainian folk building is illustrated in the bunkhouse. An apparently careless stack of lumber leaning against the side of the building is in fact a very deliberate feature. The lumber funnels smoke discharged from the oven inside, up

nearby church / Negrych cemetery

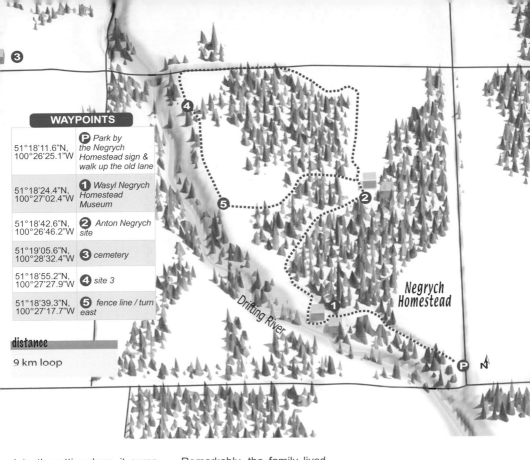

WAYPOINTS	
51°18'11.6"N, 100°26'25.1"W	**P** *Park by the Negrych Homestead sign & walk up the old lane*
51°18'24.4"N, 100°27'02.4"W	**1** *Wasyl Negrych Homestead Museum*
51°18'42.6"N, 100°26'46.2"W	**2** *Anton Negrych site*
51°19'05.6"N, 100°28'32.4"W	**3** *cemetery*
51°18'55.2"N, 100°27'27.9"W	**4** *site 3*
51°18'39.3"N, 100°27'17.7"W	**5** *fence line / turn east*

distance

9 km loop

into the attic where it cures the meats hanging there.

The Negrych Homestead is generally recognized as the most complete and best preserved Ukrainian farmstead in Canada.

Remarkably, the family lived here well into the 1980s, without making any modern improvements.

GREY OWL'S CABIN

distance

18 km loop

Riding Mountain Nat'l Park

Grey Owl's Cabin Trail

some history

This hike explores the life and times of Grey Owl, one of our more colourful historical figures. In any age, Grey Owl a.k.a. Archie Belaney would be described as an interesting character. He certainly was a complex individual. For much of his life he lived a complete lie and upon his death was exposed as a fraud and a scoundrel.

As a child, Archie immersed himself in tales of the wild west and dreamed of becoming a 'red Indian' sharing his life with forest and stream. At age 16, he emigrated from his home in England to the Canadian wilderness where a native prospector took him in, taught him how to trap and trained him as a wilderness guide. He learned the language and ways of the Ojibway people and assumed a native identity, even colouring his skin and dying his hair black. He wrote stories of life in the wilderness, glorifying the 'noble savage'. He was able to fool even those closest to him and went on to achieve international celebrity status, giving lectures across North America and Europe on native

Christel Bischoff

Christel Bischoff

ways and wisdom.

Grey Owl could be dismissed as a charlatan and a phony, but this eccentric Englishman succeeded in focusing world attention on the plight of wild animals and wild spaces and was a pioneer conservationist.

He was also the first naturalist hired by the Canadian Parks Service. He moved here in 1931, into this cabin on Beaver Lodge Lake and soon adopted and shared his home with two beavers which he named Rawhide & Jelly Roll. He was given the title "caretaker of park animals" and in one of the earliest efforts to promote conservation, he took on the task of educating park visitors.

The cabin is recognized as a federal heritage building and inside there is an excellent display of photos and letters from Grey Owl's time in the park. As well, if you look closely you can see where his pet beaver chewed into the cabin walls.

what's special

In the 1930s, Grey Owl received international acclaim as a great naturalist, a successful author, a gifted orator and a respected native spokesman. This pleasant trail winding through hills and dense forest takes you out to his beautifully preserved cabin on Beaver Lodge Lake.

OLD FORT ELLICE

some history

trade. From the 1840s to the 1880s, this was a major provisioning post. All trails led to Fort Ellice - from Saskatchewan, from Fort Pelly in the north, from Fort Garry in the east, this was a central location and had many guests.

Fortunately for these travellers, Fort Ellice was also renowned for its fine hospitality. The company men kept cows for milk and butter and tended an excellent vegetable garden. Fresh deer and buffalo meat, wild fruit, fresh vegetables and goldeye from the Assiniboine River were regularly served up to visitors who for months or even years had subsisted on nothing more than pemmican.

Two different forts, both called Fort Ellice, were built here by the Hudson's Bay Company, the first one in 1831. This was considered an ideal location as the area was a rich fur bearing land and also near the buffalo. As well it was close enough to the U.S. border to prevent the Americans from moving north and capturing the lucrative fur

Back in the 1960s, this site was home to an amusement park replete with rodeos, sky divers and baseball tournaments that attracted as many as 10,000 people at a time. As you hike south from the cairn you'll notice bits and pieces of old buildings and a wading pool - remnants of those glory days.

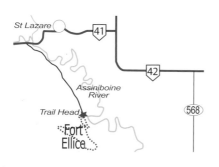

how to get there

Travelling west on Hwy 42, drive through the town of St Lazare and after crossing the Assiniboine River make a left turn onto a road that will take you south approx 4 km. Stop at the 'No Trespassing' sign & cattle gate and park to the side of the road. Phone & advise landowner Marcel Fouillard 204-683-2208 / 204-821-5112.

Our hike circles a high plateau overlooking the steep plunging valleys of the Assiniboine River & Beaver Creek and explores a legendary site as famous for its beauty as its fascinating history.

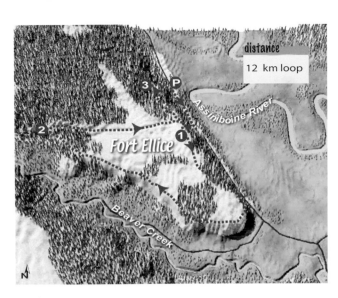

distance

12 km loop

WAYPOINTS

50°24'52.9"N, 101°17'17.9"W	**P** Park to the side of the road
50°24'41.2"N, 101°17'16.4"W	**1** Fort Ellice cairn
50°24'36.9"N, 101°18'46.3"W	**2** Turn east
50°24'52.8"N, 101°17'28.4"W	**3** descend valley to road

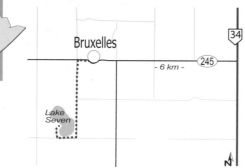

what's special

This hike begins in the tiny hamlet of Bruxelles, nestled high up in the Pembina Hills. It takes a quiet dirt road across the rolling countryside out to scenic Lake Seven.

what's special

5.6 km one way / 11.2 km out & back

some history

Mark Ably, a writer and world traveller, returned to the prairies in 1985 and wrote about the hills around Bruxelles in his book 'Beyond Forget'. He describes the strong European flavour and stark beauty of the place. "I could have been sitting in Europe ..with my bottle of vin de pays, a hunk of cheese... No wonder the French settled here."

When Manitoba was established in 1870, the proportion of French and English populations was essentially equal. There was a general assumption that Manitoba would retain this duality and continue to attract French speaking settlers. This assumption soon proved incorrect, as three demographic trends completely transformed the situation. The first was the large-scale movement of settlers from Ontario, which poured 50,000 English Protestant farmers into our province. The second wave brought the Mennonites and Icelanders. Then many Metis withdrew to better hunting in Saskatchewan.

Archbishop Tache saw these three trends as a threat to the Catholic Church and set about to redress the balance. He organized a 'Colonization Society' to entice French Catholic settlers here. The first were brought to the St Leon area around 1878. Later families were settled in the St Alphonse and St Lupicin area. By 1892, when the Belgian colonists settled at Bruxelles, they were assured the support of a close knit network of Catholic communities.

The church played an especially important role in these settlements. Priests received and placed the settlers, helping them with land titles and assuring them of being among their own kind and part of a Catholic parish.

The church remains central to the district to this day as do many Belgian traditions which have been kept alive throughout the century. One very important tradition is the love of music. Belgian music always featured a great brass band and the Bruxelles Brass

Band, established in 1899, can be seen out in full force at most any civic celebration.

STONEWALL QUARRY

distance

1.25 km loop

what you'll find

Today you can view the effects of almost one hundred years of quarrying activity. A foot path circles past the remnants of exposed limestone ledges, butte formations, excavations and a quarry pond. Dominating the landscape are three massive "draw" kilns, as well as the ruins of early "pot" kilns used in the limestone burning process.

Interpretation signage along the trail and at the Visitor Centre, provide information regarding the history of limestone quarrying, the lifestyle of the early quarry workers, the history of the region's precontact Native peoples, as well as the geology and natural history of the area.

some history

Stonewall Quarry Park commemorates the important role of limestone to the town and its development. The quarries began operation in the early 1880s with a focus on the production of quicklime. The process involved blasting limestone from the bedrock and then breaking it into smaller pieces. These smaller pieces were heated in the kilns and the result was a powder known as quicklime. The whiteness of this product placed it in high demand for use in plasters.

what you'll find

This self-guiding Trail provides a glimpse of the island's past. Parking is provided next to the village wharf and behind the community hall, so you can visit the Tomasson's Boarding House and the Dockside Fish Station before starting out on the trail. It begins near the ice house north of the dock, follows the lakeshore as far as the church, and then returns past the store and school.

distance

1 km loop

some history

The maritime beauty and remote location of this island help explain its appeal to its earliest settlers. In the early 1870s, thousands of Icelanders were forced to abandon their homeland. They were fleeing the volcanic eruptions on Mount Hecla that had spewed lava eight centimetres deep over 2500 square miles. Many came to Canada and settled on Hecla Island and the nearby western shores of Lake Winnipeg where, in 1875, they founded the Republic of New Iceland. The tiny colony lasted for six years before being absorbed into the expanding province of Manitoba, but the Icelanders remained apart from the rest of the world.

A small ferry from Hecla to the mainland began operation in the 50s but until a causeway was built in 1972, the island existed in splendid isolation, so much so that Icelanders are amazed by the purity of the language still spoken by the descendents of those original settlers.

Only a handful of people now live all year in what was once a vibrant fishing community of 500. Many had left by 1969 when Hecla was designated a provincial park, but fishermen continue to earn a livelihood from the waters around the island.

RAE TRAIL

to Austin & Hwy #1

Ladysmith Rd

Wildlife Mgmt Area

Rae Trail

34

Assiniboine River

N

to Holland & Hwy #2

distance

14 km loop

what's special

This hike is simply the best! It snakes through secluded rolling woodland interspersed with a succession of lush wildflower meadows. The scenic overlooks are a revelation. At certain spots you can see the course of the Assiniboine River twisting and turning for miles. This trail is a 'must see' and the '100 Steps' lookout point is spectacular.

This Wildlife Management Area was once home to the Rae Ski Trail which was built by a group of ski enthusiasts in the 1970s. Today, the skiers are gone and we, the Prairie Pathfinders, have developed and marked a hiking route through the area using a bit of the original ski trail. Mainly it's on old cart tracks. This is one of our very favourite trails and its stewardship is a labour of love. If you enjoy the trail and want to help out, you're welcome to join our annual trail maintenance work party. Check our website for information.

The name Rae came from the district's first settler Tom Rae, who moved here in 1891. In the years before the bridge was built, the ferry on the Assiniboine was called Rae's Ferry and some of our trail follows the cart tracks

used by early settlers to reach that ferry. Rae farmed here for nine years, until 1900 when he was struck by lightning and killed, leaving a wife and three children. Mrs. Rae, born Lizzie Mooney, was the elder sister of Nellie Mooney, the author who achieved international recognition as Nellie McClung.

FYI

Find and park by the old Rae Trail ski trail sign just off Hwy 34 about 1 km south past Ladysmith Rd or 2.5 km north of the river.

We have 2 out-houses on the trail. Find one at the east end of the loop at point ❺. The other is near the parking area ℗.

WAYPOINTS

49°43'13.7"N, 98°54'17.5"W	℗ Rae Trail sign		49°43'54.5"N, 98°56'34.0"W	❹ trail intersection
49°42'40.0"N, 98°55'18.6"W	❶ trail intersection		49°43'33.3"N, 98°56'37.8"W	❺ overlook & outhouse
49°43'29.1"N, 98°56'07.2"W	❷ trail intersection		49°43'31.6"N, 98°56'28.8"W	❻ trail intersection
49°43'07.5"N, 98°56'28.4"W	❸ Murray Hill overlook		49°43'24.5"N, 98°56'36.5"W	❼ '100 Steps' Overlook

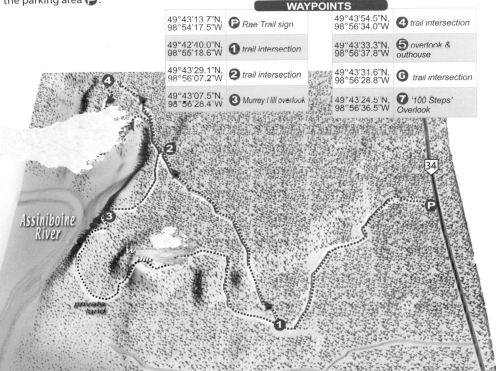

Assiniboine River

private land

KETTLE STONES

distance

4 km loop

what's special

Extremely rare kettle stones up to 15 feet in diameter

some history

Kettle stones are extremely rare. They are found in only three places in the entire world. Since their emergence here 8500 years ago, only weather has altered their appearance. These stones were formed millions of years ago when Manitoba was covered by a warm saltwater sea. At one time people thought they were plant fossils, dinosaur eggs, or even terrestrial debris - but by studying their chemical makeup, scientists have determined that they were formed from soft mud at the bottom of the sea. Bacteria, feeding on organic material in the mud caused a chemical reaction that created calcite crystals (calcite is the main ingredient in limestone). The crystals grew from the centre out in all directions, creating a ball. This rock is the kettle stone. They range in size from 45 cm to 4.5 m (18" - 15 ') in diameter and 2.5 to 3.5 m (8'-12') in height. Some are in meadows and others are amid the area's mixed forest. Some actually support full grown trees.

FYI

Road access to Kettle Stones Park is now owned by Wuskwi Sipihk First Nation. Before starting your hike you'll need to ask permission from Land Officer, Craig Stevens 204.236-4201.

Much of the road into the park (after you leave PR#268) is in very rough shape. You really need to be driving an all-wheel-drive, high clearance vehicle - a truck is best.

distance

19.8 km one way / 39.6 km out & back

This is a wide & fairly flat trail with a crushed rock surface. We recommend hiking one way by taking two vehicles and leaving one at either trailhead.

OR Begin at the north east end and hike as far as the cemetery **1** and return for a hike that's approx 8 km.

what you'll find

Beginning at the group use / camp ground at the north-east end, the first 9 km closely hugs the shoreline passing the remains of several Icelandic homesteads along the way.

You have two route choices for heading inland. If conditions are wet, it's best to take the southern part of the loop. The more direct route is sometimes under water due to beaver activity.

Much of the route to the marsh is a wide track on old roads. The last section follows the Grassy Narrows dikes. It's quite pleasant nonetheless and you'll find a wonderful profusion of wildflowers. We saw at least two dozen varieties in June, including blue flag iris (pictured at left) and yellow lady slippers.

The trail is well marked and there are excellent interpretive signs along the way, most of it focusing on the wolves of Hecla Island.

distance

5 km one way / 10 km out & back

Riding Mountain Nat'l Park

10

5

19

N

- 3 mi / 5 km -

- 3 mi / 5 km -

- 3 mi / 5 km -

Little Bald Hill Trail

19

5

N

what's special

It's impossible to exaggerate the WOW factor here. Towering 250 feet above the creek this steep sided shale hilltop provides, without a doubt, the most spectacular scenery in the province, especially in the fall.

Gazing off to the east, you have that classic Escarpment view of checkerboard farmland below. But nowhere else is that view framed to such perfection. This hike comes with our highest rating. It's a 'must see'!

FYI

The trail is well marked except for the turn-off to the Little Bald Hill. Without a GPS handy you could miss this monkey trail which may require some bushwacking if it's overgrown. This side trail is not maintained by the park.

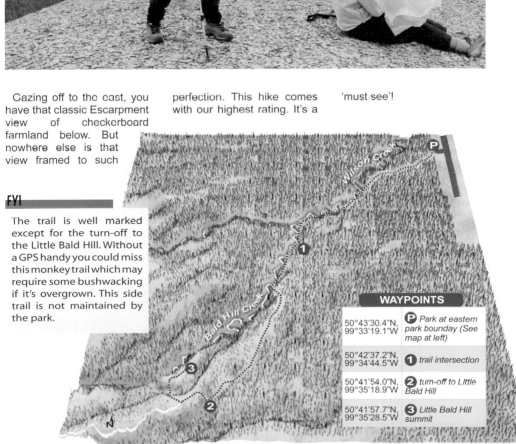

WAYPOINTS

50°43'30.4"N, 99°33'19.1"W	**P**	Park at eastern park bounday (See map at left)
50°42'37.2"N, 99°34'44.5"W	**1**	trail intersection
50°41'54.0"N, 99°35'18.9"W	**2**	turn-off to Little Bald Hill
50°41'57.7"N, 99°35'28.5"W	**3**	Little Bald Hill summit

how to get there

After leaving Hwy#10, travel 6 miles on PR#279, then turn north onto gravel road 165W. Take this road for about 2 1/2 miles, then park and walk the rest of the way, crossing a wooden bridge over the Bowsman River and climbing the hill.

At this point the road turns east and is the boundary road for the Porcupine Provincial Forest. You want to turn west (left) into a clearing. From here an old cart track leads to the north and then west, skirting the river and climbing to the overlook site.

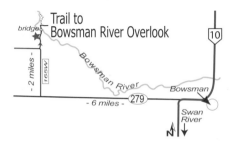

Trail to
Bowsman River Overlook

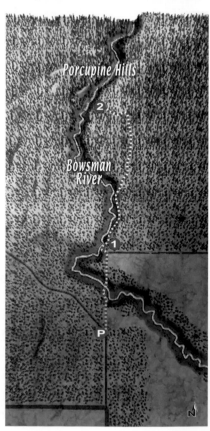

distance

3.2 km one way / 6.4 km out & back

what you'll find

A pleasant track through healthy forest with wild flowers everywhere and scenic valley overlooks. This is a popular spot with the locals. You're likely to encounter someone on horseback or an ATV, especially in berry season.

some history

Many of the locals have fond childhood memories of coming up to 'Pike's Peak' for a Sunday outing to pick saskatoons or pin cherries. From the lookout there is a stunning view of the Swan River Valley to the south.

This well defined cart track is an old logging road dating back to the early 1900s. Each spring, logs cut in the Porcupine Forest were rolled down the steep valley walls into the river where high water carried them to sawmills in Bowsman and Swan River.

WAYPOINTS		
52°16'00.9"N, 101°23'41.0"W	**P**	Park & continue north by foot
52°16'31.3"N, 101°23'42.8"W	**1**	1st overlook
52°17'22.3"N, 101°23'48.5"W	**2**	Destination overlook

NATIONAL FOOTPATH

distance

6.4 km one way / 12.8 km out & back

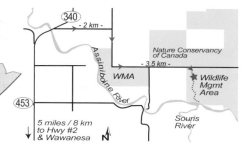

how to get there

You're looking for a sandy cart track and with no signage to help out, it's fairly complicated to find. The best approach is to leave Hwy340 just north of the Assiniboine River and travel east for 2 km, then south to the bend in the road and east again for 3.5 km. Turn off onto the cart track and continue on foot.

some history

The Prairie Pathfinders have a number of aspirations for the future but this is probably our most ambitious. This pathway along the Assiniboine River represents step one in our dream to build one continuous footpath across our province - a west-east footpath that will be the Manitoba link of Canada's National Hiking Trail.

The National Hiking Trail which has been under development since 1971 will eventually be a 10,000 km footpath across Canada. This is not to be confused with the highly publicized Trans Canada Trail which is multi-use. The National Hiking Trail is for foot travel only and is for the most part a narrow, natural-surface trail requiring little or no maintenance. The prime virtue of this trail is that it protects our heritage of natural

landscapes and provides passage, habitat, and refuge for wildlife. Typically it follows a particular landform showcasing an area of scenic interest. Ontario's Bruce Trail, which follows the beautiful Niagara Escarpment, is the best example of this and in fact is the model for National Hiking Trail development. Since its completion in 1967, the Bruce Trail has successfully preserved an area of spectacular beauty for all to enjoy.

We hope to do the same with our Assiniboine River valley and hopefully part of the Manitoba Escarpment as well. Our long-held vision of the National Hiking Trail

49°40'47.4"N, 99°34'24.3"W	**P**	*Turn off gravel road & park*
49°40'01.7"N, 99°34'05.6"W	**1**	*Mouth of Souris River Overlook*
49°39'23.1"N, 99°31'37.9"W	**2**	*Overlook*
49°39'13.3"N, 99°31'27.8"W	**3**	*Riverbend Overlook*
49°39'14.8"N, 99°31'06.5"W	**4**	*Turn around point*

in Manitoba has a pathway running along the banks of the Assiniboine River from the mouth of the Souris east and connecting up with hiking trails in Spruce Woods Park, then further along to the Rae Trail. As well, we see it extending west through to Brandon and beyond to link up with the Silverbend Trail at Miniota and Old Fort Ellice at St Lazare.

These are big dreams but we feel the time is right for this ambitious project. We will need a great deal of help to make this dream a reality but already a good number of people are volunteering their time and resources. The reader is welcome to do the same. Our immediate goal is to plot and mark a track that runs through to Spruce Woods Park by fall 2007.

Check our progress and watch for further developments on our website prairiepathfinder.mb.ca.

ROARING RIVER

what's special

A true wilderness adventure! You'll trek through dense forest dotted with beautiful upland meadows, vivid with lush green grasses and strewn with wild flowers throughout spring and summer.

Your destination is majestic Jumper Plains, a series of isolated prairies surrounded by old-growth forest.

some history

Rising above the Manitoba lowlands by some 1200 to 1700 feet, the Duck Mountains form a segment of the Manitoba escarpment and are the most prominent topographic feature in the province. About 12,000 years ago, as the last Ice Age was ending, glaciers were stalled in their retreat along these uplands. The melting ice left behind a thick blanket of clay, gravel, sand and boulder deposits resulting in an extraordinary undulating landscape adorned by lush forest and clear spring fed lakes.

The end of the Ice Age saw "the Ducks" emerge as one of the first areas of dry land. There is evidence that nomadic tribes hunted here as early as 10,000 years ago.

distance

9.25 km one way / 18.5 km out & back

how to get there

The trailhead is just off the municipal road shown on the map above. You'll find a newly cut road allowance running west about 2 km to meet up with an old pathway that skirts the Roaring River.

Some of the trails are heavily used by ATVs. As well, this area is popular with hunters. Because treaty rights allow year round hunting MB Conseration suggests wearing orange year round.

WAYPOINTS

51°53'44.2"N, 101°13'25.9"W	**P** park / begin hike
51°53'38.7"N, 101°15'17.9"W	**1** trail junction / turn south
51°51'39.4"N, 101°13'52.1"W	**2** First Prairie
51°50'56.8"N, 101°12'39.3"W	**3** Jumper Plains

what you'll find

This hike takes you into the northern part of Duck Mountain Provincial Forest, deep into the Roaring River Canyon. The route travels a combination of forestry roads and age-old foot paths. There are no trail markers. The first section of trail is a newly cut road allowance that runs west towards the river. Next you'll take up an ancient Indian path that follows the course of the waterway. This trail winds through thick forest broken by lovely open prairie and offers some lovely views of the valley.

To reach Jumper Plains you'll need to ford the river. Under normal conditions it's fairly easy to wade across, but the stoney bottom can be slippery and the water can be cold. From here, the hike out to Jumper Plains is on a narrow footpath.

Jumper Plains is a scenic treasure and a vast rolling meadow that is wonderful to explore. Plans are afoot to have this site declared an ecological reserve. This is your destination for the hike and a perfect picnic spot. Enjoy!

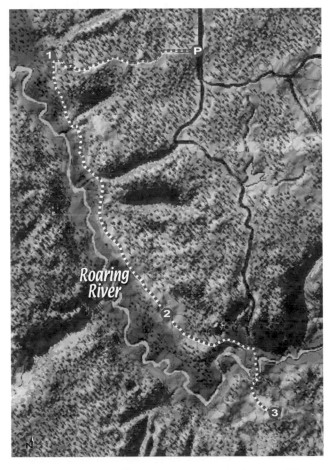

Roaring River

LANGFORD PASTURE

Frits Stevens

distance

16 km loop

what's special

This is truly an undiscovered scenic treasure! This hike weaves through pasture and thickly wooded hills on secluded old cart tracks on a beautiful stretch of terrain with some terrific overlooks.

some history

This hike takes you up on the Arden Ridge, an ancient beach ridge of Lake Agassiz that angles across the province for almost one hundred km. The Arden Ridge, described by geologists as the Upper Campbell Beach, is especially visible because Glacial Lake Agassiz stood at that water level for a fairly long time and left a lot of sand & gravel. The resulting landscape is a beautiful rolling terrain of sand dunes and forested ridges. It is truly a scenic treasure but except for the pasture manager and a few lucky cows, nobody ever sees the place. All intruders are locked out from May to October.

With its miles of fences and gates, this obviously cannot be termed pristine wilderness, but ironically this land is slowly being restored to a wild, natural state precisely because it is being used for

pasture. The 22,000 acre Langford Pasture is now owned by the Prairie Farm Rehabiltation Agency (PFRA), a federal agency formed in 1935 to rehabilitate land that had been eroded through faulty land management. It is through the enlightened practices of this agency that the growth of trees is returning to the hillsides and the once rampant erosion is now in check.

WAYPOINTS

50°9'58.4"N, 99°20'18.7"W	**P** park near pasture gate
50°9'08.6"N, 99°19'45.8"W	**1** windmill
50°8'41.1"N, 99°19'32.0"W	**2** gate
50°8'01.4"N, 99°19'05.6"W	**3** gate
50°8'10.6"N, 99°18'01.1"W	**4** gate
50°8'38.7"N, 99°17'56.7"W	**5** trail intersection
50°8'42.8"N, 99°16'25.7"W	**6** cabin / lake
50°8'42.8"N, 99°16'25.7"W	**7** gate

FYI

The pasture gates are open from the end of October to May. If you wish to obtain permission to hike in the pasture during the time the gates are locked, phone Jim Bernie, Pasture Manager (204) 476-2442. Remember to wear orange in November. This is a popular hunting spot.

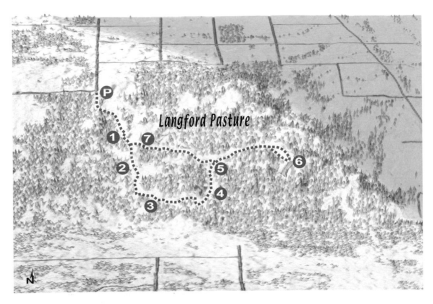

Langford Pasture

BRANDON HILLS

what's special

As you trek south along the top of the Bald Hills, you have one panoramic view after another. You can see farmland stretching as far as the city of Brandon to the north and Wawanesa to the south. It's hard to overstate the dramatic beauty of these hills. They qualify as one of Manitoba's truly secret treasures.

distance

10 km one way / 20 km out & back

what you'll find

The Brandon Hills appear on the skyline as a dark blue shoulder rising from the plains. They are an island of natural vegetation set in a sea of cultivated land and run approximately 12 km in a generally east/west direction.

Our route begins on a cross country ski trail and snakes along a south facing ridge, now and then winding out onto a grassy knoll to give you a panoramic view. For the most part, the trail is heavily wooded with poplar, burr oak and Manitoba maple. You'll encounter switchbacks, gullies and a long stretch of hazelnut. At the east end of the route you'll follow an old cart track fire road that eventually opens onto a clearing on a north facing slope. You're now on private property. This is the site of an old picnic ground and ball diamond that's been used by the locals for years

From the ball diamond, you'll continue east and climb to the bald hills on the eastern ridge. This steep eastern ridge is referred to as bald because it provides only marginal conditions for plant growth. It is exposed to wind from

Map labels:
Brandon
10
349 - 3.2 km -
- 1.6 km -
Brandon Hills
Trail Head
N

all directions and the underlying sand and gravel make the terrain too porous for trees to grow. Grasses (in one area a pinkish purple mass of little bluestem) and a profusion of wild flowers cover the ridge. Seen from a distance though, the hills appear completely barren and bald. Cattle graze along much of this area and share the path. Near the summit there are fences to keep cattle out but fence-gap stiles are provided at each end for the convenience of walkers.

some history

The old ball diamond at the north end of these hills has been a gathering place for community picnics since it was settled in 1879. The property belongs to the McPherson family. Three generations of McPhersons have been hosts to community events up here for the last 75 years and it's a great tribute to the community spirit of this

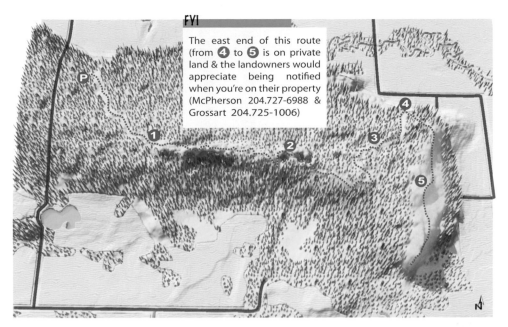

FYI

The east end of this route (from ❹ to ❺ is on private land & the landowners would appreciate being notified when you're on their property (McPherson 204.727-6988 & Grossart 204.725-1006)

WAYPOINTS

49°43'26.2"N, 99°54'33.4"W	🅿	ski trails parking
49°42'48.7"N, 99°53'37.1"W	❶	overlook / bench
49°42'44.3"N, 99°52'04.9"W	❷	tower
49°42'52.9"N, 99°50'56.0"W	❸	stile
49°43'10.5"N, 99°50'38.3"W	❹	ball park
49°42'33.9"N, 99°50'22.7"W	❺	bald hills / pasture stile

family, that they generously allow hikers and picnickers access to the glorious 'Brandon Hills'.

SUGARLOAF HILLS

distance

8.5 km one way / 17 km
out & back

P	Park at Sugarloaf Warden Station
1	beaver pond
2	beaver pond
3	junction with Central Trail
4	Sugarloaf Hills / Birdtail Bench

what's special

Catching sight of wildlife is a thrill in this wilderness setting and the panoramic views are spectacular especially with fall colours.

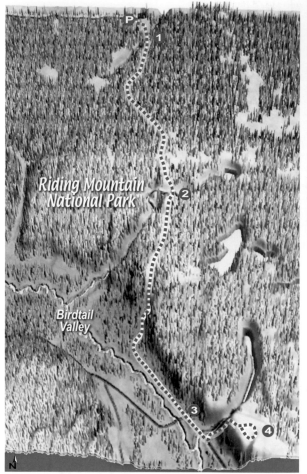

how to get there

Upon reaching the Central Trail, continue south or left on it (Sign will read To Gunn Lake) for approx 0.4 km. At this point different animal trails heading up the hills will be in sight. Pick a track and climb the slopes.

This day hike gets you into the western wilderness of this massive park on trails usually seen only by backpackers and horseback riders. It gives you a perfect taste of this scenic upland terrain.

In September 2005 we walked in here with a group and climbed up into these hills to have our lunch. It was a picture perfect day and the colours around us were so fabulous that we literally sat in stunned silence. The remoteness and seclusion of this area make it a prime destination for viewing wildlife and the park is home to some of the largest elk, moose, and black bears on the continent.

Fall is absolutely the best time to hike in here and if you're here on an early autumn morning, you'll probably hear the bugling of elk. As well, with a bit of exploring you may turn up elk antlers that are scattered throughout these hills.

some history

The Routledge Hills are remnants of a delta formed as the Assiniboine River flowed into Glacial Lake Souris. This is a large area of relatively intact natural vegetation and the open to partially stabilized dune system of these hills is an ideal habitat for the western spiderwort. This flower was designated as threatened by the Manitoba Endangered Species Act in 1994. The Routledge Sand Hills location in Manitoba represents the largest western spiderwort population in Canada.

The western spiderwort is a perennial with flowers that are usually blue or purple. Flowers appear in late June to early July. As well, some of the rare and uncommon birds found in the area include the Baird's sparrow, the ferruginous hawk, the burrowing owl and the loggerhead shrike.

western spiderwort - Photo courtesy of Glen Suggett

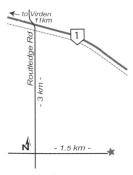

what you'll find

This is another special little corner of our province that only the locals know about. We were introduced to these hills in 2006 by one of our club members, a Virden resident. It's a great place to explore and we're told that birders come here from miles around.

Our route is a 10 km loop through rolling terrain that varies from dense forest to sandy mile roads along cultivated fields. Although ATVs and dirt bikes are chewing up the area to a frightening degree, the Bosse Hill overlook remains a particularly scenic landmark.

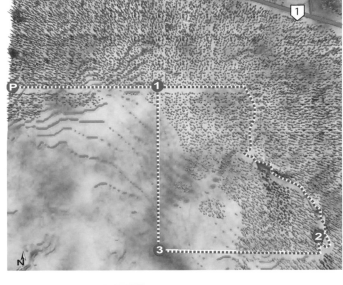

WAYPOINTS		
49°46'08.0"N, 100°46'53.9"W	**P**	park / begin hike
49°46'07.8"N, 100°45'31.6"W	**1**	trail intersection
49°45'17.4"N, 100°44'04.0"W	**2**	overlook point
49°45'15.0"N, 100°45'31.1"W	**3**	turn north

distance

10 km loop

LAUDER SAND HILLS

some history

Long before settlers arrived, these hills were marked on old maps as sand dunes. They seem a strange misfit in the middle of the prairie. In fact, the Lauder Sand hills are remnants of an ancient glacial river delta, formed many thousands of years ago. Some of the large hills are composed of pure sand. Today they're covered with creeping juniper and sand heather, which thrive in this environment. Over the centuries, grass, scrubby trees, poplar and oak have become established on most of the hills but the odd slope still has a side wall of sheer sand.

what's special

This is a fun place to explore and the sandy paths are a good choice in wet weather. In early summer two or three species of cacti can be found blooming.

WAYPOINTS		
49°28'23.4"N, 100°42'14.5"W	**P**	park beside WMA sign / begin hike
49°28'24.3"N, 100°40'40.3"W	**1**	turn south
49°27'31.9"N, 100°40'18.5"W	**2**	turn west & follow road back to **P**

finding the trailhead

This is a complicated route. The most easily explained directions have you leaving Hwy#21 north of Hartney, then travelling west on PR#541. At the 4 mile point the road number changes to PR#254. Continue on 254 as per the map, turning south for a mile, at which point you will leave 254 and continue south for 1 more mile then turn left or east for about 1 km. You'll see a sign indicating that you're in a Wildlife Management Area.

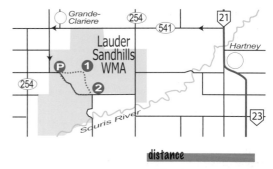

distance

7 km loop

A

Adam Lake 92–93
Agassiz Interpretive Trail 128
Amisk Trail 131
Ancient Beach Trail 37
Ancient Valley Trail 125
Asessippi 142–143
Asessippi Provincial Park 125
Assiniboine River 72–73, 102–103, 125, 134–135, 148–149, 154–155

B

backpacking 102–111
Baldy Mountain Trail 114
Bald Hill Trail 107
Beaches, The 36–37
Bead Lakes Trail 122
Bellsite 20–21
Big Rock 14–16
Birdtail Bench 107
Birdtail Trail 107
Black Lake 90–91
Black Wolf Trail 157
Blue Lakes Trail 38–39
Boreal Trail 118
Bowsman River Overlook 160–161
Brandon 72–73
Brandon Hills Trail 168–169
Bruxelles 150

C

Camp Morton 136–137
Carman 54–55
Castle Rock 82–83
Centennial Trail 78–79
Central Trail 107
Chatfield 33–34
Clearwater Caves Provincial Park 130
Clear Lake North 80–81
Clear Lake South Trail 40–41
Copernicus Hill Trail 133
Criddle / Vane Homestead 138–139

D

Dauphin 74–75
Dawson Bay 14–15
Disappearing Lakes Trail 123
Duck Mountain Forest 111–112
Duck Mountain Provincial Forest 110–111, 165–166
Duck Mountain Provincial Park 35, 39–40, 114, 129, 133

E

Elk Island 96–97
Emerson 58–59
Epinette Creek 102–103

F

Falcon Lake 17
Fire of 83 Trail 132
Flin Flon 52–53
Forester's Footsteps Trail 120
Fort Dufferin 58–59
Fort Ellice 148–149

G

George Lake 86–87, 108–109
Gorge Creek 98–99
Grand Beach 36–37
Grasshopper Valley 94–95
Grass River 104–105, 127
Grass River Provincial Park 117
Grey Owl's Cabin Trail 146–147

H

Hecla/ Grindstone Provincial Park 157
Hecla Island 28–29, 157
Hecla Village Trail 153
Hogsback 12
Hunt Lake 100–101

I

Isputinaw Trail 115

J

J.E.T. Trail 107
James Lake 92–93
Jumper Plains 165–166

K

Karst Springs Trail 117
Kettle Stones Provincial Park 156
Kwasitchewan Falls 104–105

L

Lake Audy 94–95
Lake Manitoba 44–45
Lake Minnewasta 64–65
Lake Winnipeg 76–77, 136–137
Langford Pasture 166–167
Lauder Sand Hills 174
Lester Beach 36–37
Little Bald Hill Trail 158–159

M

Manitoba Escarpment 20–21, 24–25, 64–65, 98–99
Mantario Trail 82–83, 109
Marshs Lake Trail 126
Mars Hills 18–19
Miniota Trail 134–135
Minnedosa 60–61
Morden 64–65

N

Narcisse Snake Dens 124

National Footpath 162
National Hiking Trail 162–163
Neepawa 50–51
Negrych Homestead 144–145
Newfoundland Trail 102–103
Nopiming Provincial Park 90–91, 119, 132
North Escarpment Trail 107

O

Old Fort Ellice 148–149
Old Pinawa Dam Trail 141

P

Packhorse Trail 107
Pembina Valley Park 30–31
Pinawa 56–57
Pinawa Channel 141
Pinawa Dam Heritage Park 141
Pine Point Rapids Trail 46–47
Pisew Falls 104–105
Poole Property 13
Poplarfield 33–34
Porcupine Provincial Forest 20–21, 160
Portage la Prairie 66–67
Prairie Shore Nature Trail 116
Prime Meridian Trail 32–33

R

Rae Trail 154–155
Red River 58, 68–69
Riding Mountain National Park 80–81, 94–95, 98–99, 106–107, 118, 122, 146–147, 158, 158–159, 170, 170–171
Roaring River Canyon 164–165
Roseau River 22–23
Roseisle 24–25
Routledge Sand Hills 172–173

S

Sandilands 34
Selkirk 68–69
Senkiw Bridge 22–23
Shell River 142–143
Shell River Loop Trail 125
Shell River Valley Trail 35
Shining Stone Trail 38–39
Silverbend Trail 134–135
Snow Valley 24–25
Souris 70–71
Souris Riverbend 26–27
South Cypress TCT 85
Spirit Sands Trail 42–43
Spray Lake Trail 129
Spruce Grove Nature Trail 49
Spruce Woods Provincial Park 12, 85, 102–103, 115, 126
Spur Woods 48
Stanley Trail Group 84

Stephenfield Provincial Park 121
Stonewall Quarry Trail 152
St Ambrose 44–45
St Lupicin 24–25
Sugarloaf Trail 107, 170–171
Swan River Valley 9, 161

T

Thompson 62–63
Thunder Hill 8–9
Tiger Hills 88–89
Tilson Lake Trail 107
Tinker Creek 84
Top of the World 17
Trans Canada Trail 18, 22–23, 57, 84, 85, 141, 143
Turtle Mountain Conservation District 13
Turtle Mountain Provincial Park 92–93, 123

V

Victoria Beach 76–77

W

Walk On Ancient Mountains Trail 119
Wasagaming 40–41
Wekusko Falls Provincial Park 127
West Hawk Lake 100–101
Whiteshell Provincial Park 46–47, 78–79, 82–83, 86–87, 100, 108–109, 120, 131
William Lake 10–11